GW00707394

My Dwarf Clawed Frog

by Frank Schäfer

Disclaimer of liability:
While every effort has been made to ensure that the information in this book is accurate, the author and publisher disclaim all responsibility for any errors. In purchasing this book the owner expressly accepts this disclaimer of liability.

All rights reserved. No part of this book may be reproduced, stored in any data retrieval system, photocopied or copied by any other method (electronic or otherwise), used for broadcasting or public performance, without the express permission of the publisher.

My Dwarf Clawed Frog / F. Schäfer. - Rodgau: A.C.S. (Aqualog minis)
NE: Schäfer, F. (2003)
ISBN 3-936027-30-7
German edition: ISBN 3-936027-29-3
Dutch edition: ISBN 3-936027-31-5
Swedish edition: ISBN 3-936027-33-1
© 2003 by Verlag A.C.S. GmbH (AQUALOG), Liebigstraße 1, D-63110 Rodgau /Germany

phone: +49 (0) 6106 690 140
fax: +49 (0) 6106 644 692
e-mail: info@aqualog.de
website: http://www.aqualog.de

Text, research, editing, photo selection, layout, and titling: Frank Schäfer
English translation: Mary Bailey
Business Manager: Ulrich Glaser sen.
Printing, typesetting, processing:
Lithos: Verlag A.C.S.
Printing: Westermann Druck Zwickau
Printed on Magnostar gloss, 100% chlorine-free, environmentally friendly paper.
PRINTED IN GERMANY

Literature:
Most of the used literature is credited with complete bibliography in the text. Beside this, the following title was found to be very helpfull for research:

Herrmann, H.-J. (1994): Amphibien im Aquarium. Verlag Eugen Ulmer, Stuttgart. ISBN: 3-800-7287-9

All photos are from the Aqualog photo archives, except page 5 (Noble), 10 (Lamboj), 17, 18, 20 (Tropica), 30 (Osterdal & Olsson), 34, 43, 47, 54-59, 63, 64 (inlet), 66, 67 (Herrmann, Archiv Tetra Verlag), 48 (Haupt), 60 (Arnoult & Lamotte).
All enquiries regarding photos should be directed to Bildarchiv Hippocampus, www.hippocampus-bildarchiv.de

Photographers: Burkard Migge, Shuzo Nakano, Hans Joachim Richter, Frank Schäfer, Frank Teigler und Naoto Tomizawa.

Contents

The blue pages

On the blue pages you will find general information relevant to the aquarium hobby. If you already have fish-keeping experience you can skip them.

But we have chosen this method because we have no idea what you already know, and constant references to other literature are not much help.

Claws - but no tongue

There are three orders of amphibians: the Anura (or Batrachia) to which the toads and frogs belong; the Urodela (or Caudata), to which the newts and salamanders are assigned; and the feetless Gymnophiona. Almost all the species of all three orders can be kept in a terrarium or aqua-terrarium, i.e. a container which includes a land component.

However, a small number of species from each order have adapted to a permanent life in water, and are therefore popular to a greater or lesser degree as aquarium occupants. *Typhlonectes compressicauda*, which is generally sold in the trade under the misleading name of "blind eel", is a permanently aquatic amphibian of this type, and at the same time the only member of the Gymnophiona of vivarium significance.

Of the permanently aquatic Urodela, the largest salamander in the world, the Chinese giant salamander (*Andrias davidianus*) and the Mexican axolotl (*Ambystoma mexicanum*) are particularly worthy of mention, and the latter is also kept and bred in domestic aquaria.

A few Anura have also permanently abandoned life on dry land. Lake Titicaca, in the Andes of South America, is home to remarkable frogs, the up to 30 cm long *Telmatobius* species. They are adapted to the low temperatures (11-14 °C) of this high altitude lake and are not at present maintained by aquarists.

There are further purely aquatic frogs, equally unimportant from a vivarium viewpoint, but one family, the Pipidae, has fascinated naturalists and aquarists alike. A few species, the clawed frogs (*Xenopus, Silurana*) and the dwarf clawed frogs (*Hymenochirus, Pseudhymenochirus*) have black pointed claws on the inner toes of each hind foot, with which large specimens can scratch vigorously.

Typhlonectes compressicauda, usually imported from Colombia.

This book will deal with these African species and their close relatives, the Surinam toads from South America, in which in some species the young develop in honeycomb-like brood chambers on the back of the female.

Axolotls are sexually mature larvae, a phenomenon known as neoteny. The Mexican name axolotl means "water dog".

The dwarf clawed frogs have been known to science for a long time. The first species, *Hymenochirus boettgeri*, was described by TORNIER as long ago as 1896, followed in 1906 by a second species, *H. feae* BOULENGER, then *Pseudhymenochirus merlini* CHABANAUD, 1920. In 1924 NOBLE described *Hymenochirus curtipes*, followed by *H. boulengeri* DE WITTE, 1930, while in 1957 the final form known to date was described as *H. boettgeri camerunensis* by PERRET & MERTENS.

From an aquarium viewpoint, however, these dainty little frogs crept in via the back door. Unlike many new imports among the fishes, the first importation created no great stir. For this reason I don't actually exactly when the first *Hymenochirus* reached Europe. These frogs are not yet mentioned in the standard work on reptile and amphibian maintenance, the four-volume "Terrarienkunde" by Wilhelm KLINGELHÖFFER published in 1959. I purchased my first dwarf clawed frog during the early 1970s. Because at that time I was still at school and had very little pocket money, the animal cannot have been particularly expensive. This suggests that the first importation must have been some time in the 1960s – on the quiet, so to speak, but these little frogs apparently took the hearts of aquarists by storm. The first mention of their importation known to me was in 1967 in the journal DATZ, and the first breeding report (under the erroneous name *Xenopus gilli*) was in 1969 in the same journal. Today these frogs are – quite justifiably – stocked as standard in the pet trade.

Two species of dwarf clawed frog are kept in aquaria. For practical purposes there is no difference between them as they are very similar to each other. The first is *Hymenochirus boettgeri*, Böttger's dwarf clawed frog. Compared with the second species, *H. curtipes*, the compressed dwarf clawed frog, it has rather long hind legs. But because this is evident only if both species are seen together, it is better to look at the flanks: the warts on the skin of the flanks are strikingly enlarged in *H. boettgeri*, but, by contrast, in *H. curtipes* they are the same size as those on the back. Other species and subspecies of dwarf clawed frog are not at present kept in captivity.

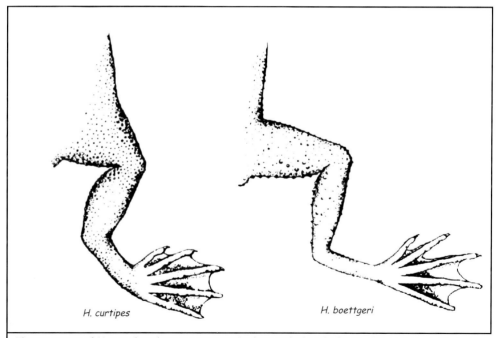

H. curtipes

H. boettgeri

The two species of *Hymenochirus* kept in aquaria can be distinguished by the length of the hind legs. These drawings originate from the original scientific description of *H. curtipes* by NOBLE, 1924.

The scientific species name

The scientific classification of the animal and plant kingdoms requires a unified system of nomenclature. Obviously animals and plants also have common names in their natural distribution areas, but these names are not governed by any rules, and so widespread species also have numerous popular names. Take the plant shown here.

It grows all over Europe, and I first encountered it as rabbit food! The English call it dandelion, a corruption of the French dent de lion, and in Germany it is Löwenzahn, in both cases meaning "lion's tooth", referring to the jagged-edged leaves. But the French also call it pis-en-lit, referring to its diuretic properties, and the Germans have a host of other names: Milchbusch (milk bush), from the milky sap that oozes from broken stems; Pusteblume (blow-flower), from the fluffy ripe seed-heads which it is such fun to blow away; and Butterblume (butter flower), a collective name for yellow-flowered plants of summer meadows.

All these names for one species, and I am sure there must be more.

It was obvious that the scientific classification of the animal and plant species of the world required a system that would permit understanding regardless of geographical boundaries. Such a system was devised by the Swedish biologist CARL VON LINNÉ (who, following the fashion of his time, preferred the Latinized version of his name, CAROLUS LINNAEUS). His basic idea was as simple as it was ingenious. First, he decreed, to be internationally valid names must be given in a dead language, as only names with no national connotations would gain international acceptance.

In addition, these names must consist of two parts. This system had already been tried and tested in the naming of humans, where each person has a personal and a family name. Linné therefore decided that closely related species should be grouped together in genera. Thus each species has a genus name followed by a species name. The genus name begins with an upper case (capital) letter, the species name with a lower case one. In addition, the name of the describer follows the species name, followed by a comma and the year of the original description. This makes it possible to locate the work in which the species was described. Thus the plant shown here is scientifically known as *Taraxacum officinale* LINNÉ, 1758.

In the wild, these two species of dwarf clawed frog inhabit the Niger and Congo basins in west and central Africa. *Hymenochirus boettgeri* is found in Nigeria, in the Democratic Republic of the Congo as far as East Congo, in western and southern Cameroon. *H. curtipes* is found to the southeast of this distribution, in the lower Congo basin.

H. boettgeri, in particular, is fairly frequently imported wild-caught. These frogs come from Nigeria and are dispatched from Lagos. But both species are as least as commonly available captive-bred. Commercial aquarium-fish breeders in both Europe and Asia produce *Hymenochirus* for the pet trade.

In the wild, dwarf clawed frogs inhabit pools in the jungle. Although these waters are generally shaded, they contain a wealth of vegetation. The water is soft and neutral to slightly acid. Water temperatures are relatively high – 24-30 °C has been recorded. The spurred clawed frog, *Silurana tropicalis*, is commonly imported together with Hymenochirus boettgeri. This indicates that they also occur together. More on *Silurana tropicalis* later in this book.

As a rule, dwarf clawed frogs can be kept in community aquaria with all sorts of small tropical fishes. They respond very well to this type of maintenance. However, they tend to breed only if they are relatively undisturbed. I have no information on the fish species that occur together with dwarf clawed frogs in the wild, and it may be that their preferred waters are in fact fish-free. However, from the biotope description, killifishes of the genera *Epiplatys* and *Aphyosemion* are to be expected, and these are also exceptionally suitable as tankmates in the aquarium.

Aphyosemion australe, the Cape Lopez killie, is well suited as a companion fish for dwarf clawed frogs.

Aphyosemion gardneri

A clawed frog biotope in Gabon

This photo, kindly supplied by Anton Lamboj, is an example of the natural habitat in which clawed frogs – in this case *Xenopus* sp. are found.

Although the dwarf clawed frogs, clawed frogs, and honeycomb toads have all made the transition to a permanently aquatic existence, unlike the majority of fishes they are still obliged to visit the water's surface regularly to take in air. The Anura breathe via lungs, not gills, and this applies to the pipids, without exception.

In fact these amphibians also obtain part of their oxygen requirement via the skin. The cleaner and more oxygen-rich the water, the less often do they need to surface and gulp air.

This process is a dangerous business for the frogs. Not in the aquarium, where nothing is likely to happen to them, but in the wild, where innumerable predators – e.g. aquatic snakes or herons - lie in wait for any tasty morsel.

For this reason the frogs must be quick in getting air. The trick is to avoid giving the enemy time to take aim. If you observe the frogs shortly after they have been moved, then you will notice the special swimming technique that they use to take a quick breath. If possible, they push off from the bottom and rapidly swim almost vertically upwards, timing their swimming movements so that they arrive with their hind legs almost extended. Once they have broken surface and taken in air, they do not allow themselves the luxury of turning round at their leisure or describing a downward curve. No, they engage reverse gear in a flash, drawing up their previously outstretched legs and extending their webs. This results in a rapid downwards movement. However, this is often no longer seen in long-established, tame individuals.

Taking in air is a dangerous matter for all amphibians that live in water. Numerous enemies lie in wait for them out of the water.

Places where cables, pipes, etc enter the aquarium are often death-traps for pipids, allowing the frogs to escape from the aquarium.

dy" and adaptable. Anyone capable of keeping a hardy fish such as the goldfish happy and healthy, will be able to cope with pipid frogs. Compared to fishes, they are highly adaptable as regards water hardness, pH, and – albeit to a far lesser extent – temperature. Moreover, these aquatic frogs are comparatively unaffected by substances that often have fishkeepers tearing their hair out, for example nitrite and nitrate. However, that does not mean that these creatures should be kept in filthy, foul-smelling conditions. But anyone with an element of fishkeeping experience can safely tackle pipids.

I have deliberately kept the heading for this chapter general. It should be obvious that a 20 cm large Surinam toad requires a different aquarium to a 2 cm *Hymenochirus*. But they do all have a few special requirements in common, and these will be covered here while the special needs of the individual species are detailed when they are discussed later on.

First it should be noted that the species commonly encountered in the aquarium are generally rather "har-

It is essential to remember the ability of these often clumsy-looking frogs to climb. In normal community aquaria this is probably the commonest cause of death. A dwarf clawed frog can even climb 10-20 cm up a vertical glass surface, pressing its moist belly against it like a sucker.

The other, larger species have greater difficulty, but are adept at using heater cables, filter hoses, etc as climbing aids. The danger of escape is particularly high during the settling-in period of newly purchased individuals, but sudden changes in the weather can provoke wanderlust even in long-established specimens.

In nature this migratory urge is often dangerous enough, in view of the legions of enemies that lie in wait for frogs. In the living-room such an excursion is almost always fatal, as the poor little creatures very quickly dehydrate in our homes, which from an ecological viewpoint are the equivalent of cold, dusty deserts. Sometimes the wanderer can be saved if it is found in time and placed in a bucket of water. But that is the exception rather than the rule. For this reason the aquarium should ideally be covered with no apertures, and instead have holes drilled in the sides to take the filter hoses.

There are very good external filters in which the heating is integrated into the filter, and these are ideal for the maintenance of pipids, as they permit a truly hermetically sealed aquarium. Always remember that every cable entering the aquarium poses a threat to the frogs. Of course, the cable apertures can be plugged with filter wool or similar, but such solutions are really not satisfactory in the long term, and also too insecure.

The filter capacity should be such as to turn over the entire volume of the aquarium once or twice per hour. Filter inlets should be carefully fitted with guards, as otherwise dwarf clawed frogs may be completely sucked in and even the larger species can suffer serious injuries.

Dwarf clawed frogs need to be kept warmer than the other species – 28 °C should be regarded as the ideal maintenance temperature. Some form of heating should be provided in every pipid aquarium. As well as the already mentioned "thermofilters" there are also heating mats that are placed under the aquarium. They too offer the advantage that the cable doesn't need to enter the aquarium. The disadvantage is that only a thin layer of sand or gravel (1-2 cm) should be placed in the aquarium if a heating mat is used, as otherwise there is a danger of heat build-up. But plants will not grow satisfactorily in such a shallow substrate, so you will have to fall back on free-floating unrooted plants, Java fern and *Anubias*, or potted plants.

Sometimes the african clawed frog, *Xenopus laevis*, does not require heating, but more of that later. Even for small species such as dwarf clawed frogs, the aquarium should not be too shallow. These creatures adopt mating positions that make a water depth of 30 cm or more desirable even for dwarf clawed frogs. The larger species require proportionately deeper aquaria, otherwise breeding will not occur.

With pipid frogs the choice of substrate is a matter of the aquarist's preference. It is all the same to the frogs. In laboratory "nurseries", where millions of clawed frogs are bred for scientific purposes, totally bare tanks with no substrate are used. So that works too, but is rather unaesthetic! Moreover the substrate is home to numerous useful micro-organisms which help keep the aquarium environment stable. Bogwood and rocks can in any case be used as decor, but rocks should not be rough or have sharp edges. Large clawed frog species have a habit of burrowing under rocks, and this can lead to a pile of rocks collapsing. For such species rocky structures should be stuck together using silicone sealant.

A standard 60 cm aquarium is quite adequate for small species (*Hymenochirus, Pipa parva, Silurana*). For other species please see the relevant chapters.

How large an aquarium

In aquarium circles there is a saying, "An aquarium can never be too large." How so? Well, the main reason is that the body of water in the aquarium is more stable, chemically speaking, the larger its volume. In other words, a large aquarium is significantly less work than a small one.

Beginners and non-aquarists often think that fishes feel like prisoners in a small aquarium. This is not the case. Compared with the wild, even a large aquarium is no more than a tiny puddle, but fishes have no more concept of freedom than do other animals - such an abstraction is of no biological relevance to them. Only mankind has an inbred desire for freedom, and even so the concept has no single definition. Just ask 10 people of your acquaintance, what they understand by "freedom". In all probability you will get 10 different answers. In actuality, Man's quest for freedom is the recipe for his evolutionary success. It is nothing more than an innate feeling of discontent with the individual's personal circumstances, in consequence of which, depending on the degree of dissatisfaction, the person concerned seeks for an opportunity to alter his or her situation. By virtue of his inventive genius Man can adapt his environment to his needs and hence survive literally anywhere. In short, the human quest for freedom is a natural species-specific survival factor.

By contrast animals, including all fishes, are incapable of adapting their environment to their needs. Instead they are dependent, for better or worse, on their ability to adapt to their present environmental conditions. A blenny that decided to abandon its troglodytic existence for the lifestyle of a herring would survive only a few hours. Thus animals have no freedom. And thus the question of how large an aquarium has nothing to do with the amount of space available to a fish in nature. The aquarist should instead ask, "Would the fish species that I want to keep colonize my aquarium if the habitat it provides occurred in the wild?"

The significant differences between an optimal aquarium and the wild are: there are no enemies; there is an unlimited food supply; there is no competition; there are no natural catastrophes (drought, flood, etc) - the aquarist ensures all these things.

Accordingly the tank size necessary is a function of the expected eventual size and the behavior of the fishes. For inactive predators, that spend the entire day lying motionless in wait for prey, the tank length should be about three times, the tank width about twice, the body length of the fish. For active shoaling fishes the rule of thumb is a tank length at least 10 times body length, and tank width five times. Finally, the number of fishes must be taken into account. And here the old aquarists rule remains valid - at least two liters of water per cm of fish length.

If you are thinking of setting up an aquarium, please always bear its maintenance requirements in mind. Every aquarium requires a weekly or fortnightly partial water change of 10-25% of its volume. This removes pollutants, the accumulated waste products from metabolic processes, and also replaces depleted trace elements. For a 1000 liter aquarium that means 200-500 liters of water to be shifted (100-250 liters out, and the same back in). As a new recruit to the hobby you will do best to start with an aquarium of 150-300 liters capacity. A tank of this size will provide a chemically very stable volume of water and is a good size for almost all the aquarium fishes normally available in the trade.

How a filter works

There are many different types of filter, all with advantages and disadvantages. Basically, every filter has a mechanical and a biological section. The former serves to remove particles – that cloud the water or are regarded as dirt - from the aquarium. For this purpose the aquarium water is drawn through a suitable filter medium and the cleansed water is then pumped back into the aquarium. This mechanical cleansing is usually achieved using filter floss, sponge, or the like. You should get into the habit of cleaning this "dirt filter" weekly during the partial water change. Ideally the filter medium should be rinsed in a bucket of newly siphoned-off the aquarium water, as this will avoid harm to the useful aerobic bacteria also contained in the medium.

The biological section is usually divided into various zones. The best-known is the aerobic zone, which endeavors to produce the largest possible population of the aerobic bacteria that convert ammonia to nitrate via nitrite, by providing a substrate with the largest possible surface area for colonization. This process is strictly oxygen-dependent. Typical substrates include ceramic tubes, "bioballs", various artificial materials, porous clay balls, and even basalt chips. The most extreme form of the aerobic filter is the so-called trickle filter, in which the water cascades over thin layers of filter media and is thus constantly supplied with abundant oxygen. This works exceptionally well, although only miserable plant growth is possible when the water is processed this way, and in addition the high oxygen level encourages rampant algal growth. For this reason such filters are best used only for heavily populated aquaria with alkaline water, where the danger of ammonia toxicity is greatest.

More and more frequently the aerobic filter indispensable in any aquarium is nowadays complemented by an anaerobic filter, inhabited by anaerobic bacteria to which oxygen is toxic.

These filters have two great advantages. Firstly they can be used to cultivate bacteria that break down the relatively harmless nitrate into gaseous nitrogen and oxygen. Both gases can then escape from the water. If the filter functions properly then it can thus be used to keep the level of nitrate in the aquarium very low. Secondly, in this type of filter the highly important plant nutrients that are oxidized by aerobic filters (and thus rendered useless to plants) undergo reduction, i.e. the oxygen is removed again. For this reason many aquarists run a slow-flow anaerobic filter in bypass, i.e. connected to the outlet of the aerobic filter.

There are various media for anaerobic filters. Special artificial media are used for the nitrate reduction filter, sold already impregnated with the required bacterial culture. As a rule a small external filter with a low throughput is used for the plant-friendly bypass filter, and filled with, for example, fine sand or special filter media such as sintered glass, etc. Your dealer will be pleased to advise on this.

The filter can also contain materials with a special purpose, for example filter carbon. This so-called activated carbon is very effective for removing some medication residues from the water, as well as yellowing and other types of discoloration. Filter carbon should be used only for a specific purpose, not on a permanent basis. In addition a bag of peat can be placed in the filter to acidify the water. There are also special ion-exchange resins, which, when necessary, can be used to bind up nitrate or phosphate, lowering levels of these pollutants quickly and effectively. Special filters filled with diatomaceous earth can be used to produce sparkling water and even reduce the number of microorganisms in the water.

Plants perform a number of functions in the aquarium. They remove pollutants, which serve them as food for growth. They provide hiding places for harassed adults and juveniles. They produce oxygen and reduce carbon dioxide levels during the day. And finally, a planted aquarium is much more attractive than a bare tank.

In practice it is important to distinguish between aquaria for dwarf forms (*Hymenochirus, Pipa parva, Silurana*) and for the larger species. Where the latter are concerned an attractively planted aquarium must remain a dream. They are too clumsy, the substrate will be dug over too much, etc, etc. But we will begin with the dwarf species, which like well-planted aquaria. In this case the aquarist can run wild and create a real underwater jungle. In principle, practically any plant cultivated in the hobby can be used in the aquarium for dwarf clawed frogs.

Choice of the correct substrate is important for a planted aquarium - it must be at least 7 cm, better 10 cm, deep. At the bottom you can use a layer of "compost" material some 1-2 cm deep. This compost must contain a long-term mineral fertilizer in the form of special clay or similar. Horticultural fertilizers and composts are totally unsuitable as these have a high content of organic nutrients that will pollute the aquarium and ruin the water quality. On top of the compost there should be a 5-7 cm layer of fine aquarium gravel, which should, as usual, be thoroughly washed before use. Finally there is the top layer, again painstakingly washed clean. Normal aquarium gravel is perfectly suitable, but you can use sand instead – it is merely a matter of personal preference.

Next carefully add just enough water to thoroughly moisten the substrate. This will enable you to plant the aquarium without a load of "dirt" floating up from the bottom layers. Once all the plants are in position, you can - carefully! - fill the aquarium with pre-warmed (to 18-22 °C) water. Finally set the filtration and heating going. Now the aquarium should remain unoccupied for at least two weeks - this is necessary to allow the aquarium to develop the population of micro-organisms needed to turn a sterile tank of water into a functional aquarium biotope. During this period the plants will start to grow and so the lighting must be turned on right away.

Dwarf clawed frogs like densely planted aquaria.

Quite different arrangements are necessary when keeping large pipid species, where in the long term we can keep only those plants that are very undemanding. Because large pipids are also greedy feeders, good aquarium hygiene is essential. Too deep a substrate is thus disadvantageous, as too much detritus will quickly accumulate in it. A substrate about 3-5 cm deep is appropriate, and, because this too will accumulate rather a lot of dirt, it should be stirred vigorously with a stick once a week .

This will prevent pockets of putrefaction from developing. The stirred up dirt is best removed by immediately performing a partial water change. Obviously only a few plant species will grow under such conditions. Species that root in the substrate should be avoided without fail. But even the aquarium for large pipids should not be devoid of plants, so I recommend the use of *Anubias* and Java fern (*Microsorium*), tied to bogwood, as decoration.

The plants, complete with wood, are then simply removed and placed in a bowl before the big weekly clean-up. Floating fern (*Ceratopteris*) will ensure biological equilibrium. This plant grows vigorously, thereby removing organics from the water, and its roots look very attractive. Other possibilities include small-leaved willowleaf (*Hygrophila polysperma*) and water wistaria (*H. difformis*) – these plants too grow well unrooted, although they require fairly intensive cultivation in the large pipid aquarium. The individual stems should be bundled together in groups of about 15, with a piece of foam about 3 mm thick separating each pair of stems, the whole held together with a rubber band (taking care not to squash the stems). Each bundle should be pushed into the substrate and held in place with a few stones. The bundle can then be removed just before the weekly clean-up.

Dwarf Anubias (*Anubias barteri* var. *nana*)

This attractive plant is one of the easiest aquarium plants of all, and can be unreservedly recommended for any aquarium. It does well attached to decor items (see "Planting plants") and will grow in acid or alkaline water, and even in dim light. Unfortunately this plant grows rather slowly, so that it is usually rather expensive to buy. The different varieties of this species differ mainly in their height: *A. barteri* var. *nana* produces leaves only 3-5 cm in length. Anubias have relatively brittle leaf stems, and, because they are longer, those of other species snap off easily if a frog charges through them.

Microsorium pteropus

Microsorium pteropus "Tropica"

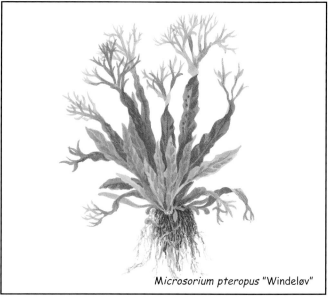

Microsorium pteropus "Windeløv"

Java fern (*Microsorium pteropus*)

Generally speaking the same applies for Java fern as for *Anubias*: this plant too will grow almost everywhere and anywhere and does well attached to rocks, etc. This fern is propagated via small plantlets that form along the edges of older leaves. There are several very attractive cultivars of Java fern, e.g. the "Windelov" and "Tropica" forms. Unlike the *Anubias*, which develops very sturdy clinging roots, the roots of Java fern are fine and form a dense, black-brown mat.

Small-leaved willowleaf

Small-leaved willowleaf, pink-veined cultivated form

Water wistaria

Small-leaved willowleaf (*Hygrophila polysperma*) and water wistaria (*H. difformis*)

Small-leaved willowleaf and water wistaria are stemmed plants and can be used in many ways in the aquarium. If they are regularly "stopped" then they will form decorative bushy growth, but if allowed to grow freely they will extend along the surface and send attractive adventitious roots down into the water. In this habit they are excellent spawning plants for many pipids. Both species are also available in colorful cultivated forms - the pink-veined form of the willowleaf is shown above right.

Floating or Indian fern (*Ceratopteris cornuta*)

No aquarium for pipids should be without floating fern, and it is just as good for the large Surinam toad (*Pipa pipa*) as for dwarf clawed frogs. It combines several advantages: firstly, it grows free-floating on the surface, and thus is in no danger of being dug up. Secondly, it grows very rapidly and in consequence removes large quantities of organic pollutants from the water.   And thirdly, it provides shade (many pipids are not too keen on bright light) and gives the frogs a sense of security – most frog predators attack from above. If the water's surface is vegetated, the frogs think they cannot be seen and hence feel safe. Floating fern has just one disadvantage: it won't tolerate strong filter currents, especially if it is constantly tumbled around in circles. If necessary the plants must be held in place with a piece of nylon fishing line, else they will die. When growing this fern and other floating plants it is sensible not to fill the aquarium to the top. Instead allow a 2-5 cm air space between the water's surface and the cover glass, and then growth will be optimal. If you have no other plants in the aquarium then relatively little light will suffice – a single fluorescent tube for 30 cm of tank depth.

Planting plants

Basically, three types of plants are cultivated in the aquarium: floating plants, stemmed, and rosette-forming plants.

The floating plants are most easily "planted". They are simply placed on the water's surface, and all that is necessary is to make sure the roots are pointing downwards - and even that is superfluous with the rootless types. All floating plants "dislike" filter currents, and it is often pointless to try and grow them in heavily filtered aquaria.

Stemmed plants form only a moderately extensive root structure. They are propagated via cuttings taken from any stems that are long enough. As a rule cuttings should be about 10 cm long. When planting stemmed plants the following points should be noted: never plant them in bundles, but insert each stem separately. The lower leaves should be removed, as if buried in the substrate they will rot and possibly infect the stem with decay. When you buy stemmed plants from an aquarium store, they will usually be clipped together with lead or planted in a small pot - the lead or pot should be removed before planting. Finally, remove any roots already present. If the lower stem looks transparent then it has been squashed - cut off the affected part with a sharp knife before planting the remainder.

Finally, the third group of plants comprises the rosette-forming types. These plants form an extensive root structure. They are propagated via runners or offsets. With these plants too, any lead strip or pot must be removed before planting, and the roots should then be gently teased out and shortened to about 3 cm long using a sharp knife. When planting, it is essential that the roots all point downwards into the planting hole - if they get bent upwards during planting then the plant will not grow well. Rosette-forming plants possess a "crown" or woody rootstock (rhizome) from which the foliage grows, and it is important to ensure that this growing point is not buried in the substrate but extends a few millimeters above it.

A number of rosette-forming plants of the genus *Anubias*, as well as ferns of the genera *Microsorium* and *Bolbitis*, do not grow well if planted in the substrate. These plants are best tied to wood or porous stones using dark cotton, and will attach themselves firmly in time. These plants can often be purchased growing on rocks or wood.

Many rosette-forming plants are marsh plants by nature, and grow submerged only part of the time in their natural habitat. To this group belong many species of the genera *Cryptocoryne* and *Echinodorus*, for example. When first planting an aquarium, these plants should generally make up only about a third of the species used. This is because these plants grow only relatively slowly. During the initial phase of a new aquarium the biological conditions are such that many undesirable algae find an optimal environment for growth.

Because aquatic plants and algae compete with one another for resources, logically fast-growing plants will be more successful than slow-growing ones. Your dealer will, of course, be pleased to advise which plants will be suited to your aquarium. But if you want an extensive discussion with your dealer it is best not to visit him during his busy period - this also applies when the object is to design a planting scheme.

Feeding dwarf clawed frogs

All adult amphibians are *carnivores* (flesh-eaters), and dwarf clawed frogs are no exception. But while all terrestrial amphibians orient, almost without exception, on the movement of their prey, in dwarf clawed frogs smell is largely used for that purpose instead. This makes feeding them relatively easy compared to terrestrial amphibians. Any commercially available frozen food suited to their mouth size will be eaten by dwarf clawed frogs. Their favorites are the various types of mosquito larvae, especially bloodworms. Good results can be obtained using this food as the basis of the diet. In addition they can be given live food in the form of *Tubifex* or water fleas (*Daphnia*).

In particular, feeding with water fleas results in a spectacle that shouldn't be missed.

Often the little frogs balance almost vertically in the water like seahorses to snap up one water flea after another. In this situation, of course, *Hymenochirus* are orienting visually. Their lateral-line organ may also play a part (more of this later).

Experience has shown that dwarf clawed frogs take flake food only reluctantly. Granular foods are better, but acceptance is a matter of individual preference. One problem of housing fast-swimming fishes with dwarf clawed frogs is that the latter are rather slow eaters. Also, often the fishes will have eaten most of the food before the *Hymenochirus* notice what is going on.

For this reason less agile fishes, such as the killies mentioned earlier, are better companions. Bloodworms and *Tubifex*, both excellent foods for dwarf clawed frogs, have a bad reputation. It is claimed that both organisms are found in heavily polluted waters and hence are unsuitable as animal foods. In the case of bloodworms this is only partially correct. In fact chironomid midges (whose larvae are termed bloodworms) are found all over the world in almost every ecosystem (from extremely clean to heavily polluted). Those collected as food originate from many different countries and have only one thing in common: I have never heard of a single case of fishes being poisoned by their use.

One thing is true, however – if the food is not kept properly frozen it can spoil. But that can happen with any frozen food.

Tubifex, on the other hand, are always indicators of massive organic pollution when found in large numbers. But even *Tubifex* can be fed without worry provided they are always thoroughly washed and only healthy, blood-red worms are used.

It is sufficient to feed dwarf clawed frogs once per day.

By and large, similar rules apply here as for dwarf clawed frogs. except that the food particles should be appreciably larger. Adults of the larger pipid species should all be fed only once every 3 to 5 days.

Suitable frozen foods include shrimps and smelt (*Osmerus eperlanus*). The flesh of warm-blooded animals, e.g. beef heart, liver, and other offal, should not be used. These types of foods are not fully digested and will badly pollute the water, not to mention the poor nutritional value these foods have for the frogs.

Fish fillets are a valuable food, available in frozen packs for human consumption. Even so this food should be offered at most every other feed, as it is very poor in roughage and also lacks certain nutrients.

It should be made a rule that leftover and regurgitated food, plus large droppings, should be removed about 2 hours after large pipids have been fed. This will help maintain the otherwise rather unstable biological balance of the aquarium.

Large pipids, unlike dwarf clawed frogs, should not normally be kept with fis-

hes. Small fishes will sooner or later be eaten, and large ones may harm the frogs. It is, however, beneficial to keep a large shoal of round-tail guppies of the wild type in the pipid aquarium.

They should not be specially fed, as it is their job to deal with leftovers.

Now and then a guppy will be eaten, but in all probability their numerous offspring will compensate for such losses.

Wild-type guppies are outstanding biological helpers in the large pipid aquarium.

Biological equilibrium in the aquarium

It is impossible to achieve a true biological equilibrium in the aquarium - that must be understood right from the start. The amount of extraneous nutrients (in the form of fish food) is simply too great. One can - and should - nevertheless endeavor to create a stable aquarium environment which must then be supported by partial water changes and filter cleaning.

The basic prerequisite for such a stable aquarium environment is the use of water of consistent initial quality. That is to say, that the water used for changes should be identical in hardness and pH with that already in the aquarium. So think this over carefully before deciding on "home-brewed" water instead of your mains water. Because you will have to prepare it yourself, week-in, week-out!

The aquarium hobby is essentially about culturing bacteria. Without these invisible helpers it is impossible to run an aquarium. On the one hand there are the nitrite-forming bacteria. Fishes constantly excrete highly toxic ammonia (from the breakdown of protein) from their gills, and this first group of essential helpful bacteria convert this ammonia into nitrite (still highly toxic, and normally lethal to fishes in concentrations of 1 mg/liter). The bacteria need oxygen to convert ammonia to nitrite, and hence are termed aerobic bacteria. The second group of bacteria that make it possible for fish to live in aquaria are also aerobic, and convert the still highly toxic nitrite into relatively harmless nitrate. When maintaining an aquarium the aim should be a nitrate level of about 30 mg/liter; the value should never be appreciably higher, but lower is OK.

It is always the same genera of bacteria that perform this important nitrification, but every aquarium will have its own "micro-climate" depending on its basic water parameters, i.e. hardness and pH. The bacteria are appreciably more sensitive than fishes to fluctuations in water parameters, hence it is immensely important always to use "matching" water for water changes.

As well as the aerobic nitrifying bacteria there are innumerable other micro-organisms, i.e. bacteria, fungi, etc, that colonize aquaria. The higher the nutrient loading of the aquarium, the higher the number of these organisms in the water. Additional factors that increase the micro-organism population include the fish population density and the amount of convertible organic material in the aquarium, i.e. the so-called mulm. Mulm consists of fish excreta, dead vegetation, uneaten food, etc, and it makes no difference whether it is lying around the tank or out of sight in the filter! The organisms that process mulm are intrinsically harmless, but if their population increases to excess then these normally harmless organisms represent a danger to the fishes. The immune systems of many fishes kept in aquaria are naturally only weakly developed, as the micro-organism population in many tropical waters is extremely low because they are very nutrient-poor. Hence it is obvious that the micro-organism population should be kept as low as possible by siphoning off mulm during water changes, filter maintenance, and sensible limitation of the fish population.

Should it be necessary, for whatever reason, to populate the aquarium densely with fishes, then a UV sterilizer, installed in the filter return, is one way of effectively reducing the number of micro-organisms in the water. But – and this is where skill comes in – the aquarist should always seek to create a degree of biological equilibrium through knowledge and thought, and use special equipment only where unavoidable.

Like all life forms, frogs can suffer from a large variety of diseases. It is sensible to have a number of medications available so that treatment can be rapid in the event of infection.

The onset of disease is almost always evident from a striking change in behavior. If a frog lies listlessly in a corner of the aquarium, exhibits unusual colors on its skin or areas of haemorrhage, eats little and without enthusiasm, then these are warning signs. Often at this early stage of the disease it is still possible to stimulate the natural immune response of the frog by performing a large water change and raising the normal maintenance temperature by 3-4 °C. Very many pathogens die or are at least severely weakened if the temperature is somewhat higher than 30 °C.

Because sick animals eat very little, they should be fed only sparingly, if at all, in order to avoid additional harm to the patients through poor water quality.

The most important method of disease treatment is prevention! This includes, of course, not just regular maintenance of the aquarium but also the quarantining of new arrivals. Never introduce a newly-purchased frog into an established population immediately. Every animal carries pathogens. This is not the fault of the breeder or dealer, it is simply the way things are. Capture, transportation, and acclimatization to different water conditions are all stressful, with negative effects on the frog. This can lead to an outbreak of disease that the frog would previously have fought off easily.

On the other hand, the frogs already swimming in your aquarium will also be carrying pathogens. The new arrival, in its weakened state, can very easily become infected and even seriously ill. The only sure way to avoid these dangers is a small extra aquarium, a so-called quarantine tank. For pipids this can be quite small – 30 x 20 x 20 cm will as a rule be adequate for dwarf clawed frogs and the juveniles (the normally available size) of other species. Of course, a 20 cm large Surinam toad (*Pipa pipa*) requires more space, but can still be quarantined in a relatively small aquarium of 60 x 30 x 30 cm (but note, only one individual per tank of this size!).

The quarantine tank should be filled with water from the main aquarium. A heater-stat and a small internal filter will complete the set-up. Don't bother with substrate or plants, which will only be a nuisance in a quarantine tank. No prophylactic medication should be used in the quarantine tank. With luck the new frog will recover very rapidly from the stress and never fall ill. All that is required is to monitor the water parameters in the quarantine tank regularly. If, after two weeks, the frog shows no obvious external signs of disease, then it can be transferred to the main aquarium.

If treatment is necessary, then again the quarantine tank offers many advantages. Firstly, much less medication is required in a small tank. Secondly, the water change required after treatment is quick and easy to carry out.
Thirdly, the treatment can be administered more precisely, as substrate, plants, and also a large filter can considerably hasten the breakdown of the active ingredients of the medication. And fourthly, the undesirable side-effects of some medications (dead snails, damaged plants, intolerance of some active ingredients by some frog species)are irrelevant in the quarantine tank.

Unfortunately it has to be said that there are only a few relatively harmless and easily treated diseases that affect pipid frogs. Moreover diagnosis is incomparably more difficult than in fishes. For this reason the generally serious diseases that affect pipids should be diagnosed and treated only by a specially trained vet. But it is worth also mentioning here that pipids only rarely fall sick at all.

Small cottonwool-like patches of fungus (*Saprolegnia*) on the skin are fairly harmless. They can be treated with one of the proprietary medications for fishes available in the trade, using the same dosage as for fishes. A helpful form of "first aid" for fungal infections and unspecified skin infections (usually appearing as light spots) is a salt bath (iodine-free cooking salt, 0.4% solution, i.e. 4 g salt per liter of water) accompanied by raising the temperature to 30 °C. Like all types of treatment, this should take place in the quarantine tank!

Bacterial diseases are dreaded and, unfortunately, difficult to treat. They typically manifest as red spots ("red-leg disease" – but not limited to the legs), i.e. areas of subcutaneous haemorrhage. The only effective treatment is antibiotics, which should be administered only under the supervision of a vet. Treatment with antibiotics is not without dangers for the aquarist, and should never – and this is no idle warning – be undertaken "off one's own bat". Bacterial diseases can also be combated without chemicals by optimizing living conditions: A1 water quality, high-protein food (especially *Tubifex*), and warmth will improve the immune response of the frog and often prove successful. Bacterial diseases are generally the result of earlier unfavorable living conditions, developing only when the frog has been weakened by other factors. The causative pathogens in such cases are often normally harmless bacteria responsible for the breakdown of dead plant and animal material. Reduction of the micro-organism population in the water via a UV sterilizer is thus a good method of prophylaxis.

In the event of a bacterial infection, always look for the root cause. Has the pH been fluctuating with the day-night rhythm? Is there a troublemaker in the aquarium, continually causing disturbance and stress? Could there be an unsuspected parasitic infestation? Is the filter properly maintained, and has a partial water change been performed every week? Is the tank overpopulated?

The frog is not ill if it loses skin. All amphibians and reptiles regularly moult their outer layer of skin in fragments. Pipids immediately eat these pieces, so the owner can often remain unaware of the moulting and panic when he first sees it. But it is harmless and perfectly normal.

I must mention a peculiarity of pipids: they can literally eat themselves to death! Newcomers to amphibian maintenance generally need to get used to the fact that their pets require relatively little food. Some dwarf clawed frogs may eat to bursting and then die, so the rule is, moderate feeding and not too often!

This is not to be confused with "dropsy", an accumulation of lymphatic fluid which can cause the frogs to swell up like balloons. The cause is the total or partial failure of the lymph heards that normally pump the fluid around. A vet can draw off fluid from the lymph sac using a fine canula and thus give the affected frog relief. Often recovery is spontaneous as the lymph heards resume their function. A cooking salt bath and raising the temperature to 30 °C is also effective for dropsy.

Pipids can be affected by all sorts of parasites (e.g. worms), protozoa, and even tuberculosis (a bacterial disease). But in all such cases only the vet can help. Don't wait too long before visiting the vet, as the sooner the treatment, the better the chance of a cure. Moreover most vets will not normally have been confronted with many sick frogs, and may need to read up in the specialist literature. This takes time.

The so-called "crowd effect" is not a disease as such but the result of overcrowding in tadpoles. It manifests as tadpoles that develop poorly or die before metamorphosis (i.e. the change from tadpole to frog), and affects all frog species. The cause is invariably overcrowding in the rearing container. It is better to rear 20 healthy frogs than 2,000 runts! Moderation is the key to animal maintenance!

In adult frogs too overpopulation is often the cause of the explosive spread of disease. True, frogs are relatively immune to pollution of the water per se, at any rate far less sensitive than fishes. But a cess-pit environment offers ideal living conditions for potential pathogens. If the frog's immune system is then weakened for whatever reason, it often falls ill very suddenly, and may infect its companions because the pathogens then multiply like wildfire. The result is an epidemic.

For this reason, when maintaining an aquarium for pipids you should employ the same high level of husbandry as for fishes – and then you will not as a rule have problems with serious disease in your pets.

Here we show you the most important diseases using the Chinese dwarf newt *Cynops orientalis*, as an example, as, luckily, our dwarf clawed frogs are all in good health. Top: dropsy; center: an individual with fungus; bottom: an individual with a severe bacterial infection.

The Tropica® Aqua Decor range consists of plants grown on roots and stones, making it easy to refresh and change the appearance of your aquarium as often as you like. The Tropica® BankWood range consists of pieces of tree root which can be attached to the panes of your aquarium with a suction cup. An entirely new dimension, offering an infinite number of decorative options.

tropica®
Aqua Decor
Tropica Aquarium Plants
Box 3 · DK-8530 Hjortshoej · Denmark
Tel.: +45 86 22 05 66 · Fax: +45 86 22 84 66
e-mail: tropica@tropica.dk ·
www.tropica.dk

TROPICA®
BANKWOOD

Chemistry - how water works

Even if you have previously regarded chemistry as not your particular cup of tea, a few basic elements of chemical knowledge will not come amiss in the aquarist.

First of all there is water hardness. Most people will already have heard of this, as water hardness is responsible for the "chalking up" of kettles, hot water pipes, etc. The concept of water hardness originates from the washing powder industry and was originally used to quantify the amount of soap powder needed to create an effective lather for washing. Only later was it discovered that it was calcium and magnesium compounds dissolved in the water that were responsible for the greater or lesser soap requirement. The terms "hard" and "soft" derive from the sensation evoked by soap lather on the skin in the water in question.

From an aquarium viewpoint it is mainly the so-called "carbonate hardness" (KH, expressed in degrees) that is important. It is a measure of the compounds calcium and magnesium carbonate, which react with carbonic acid to form calcium and magnesium bicarbonate. Because they are chemically unstable, both these substances play an important role in the aquarium. They react reciprocally with carbonic acid and can be problematical per se for so-called "softwater fishes" that practically never encounter them in nature. In addition there are yet other calcium and magnesium compounds in water, which, however, are relatively stable chemically and of no great practical significance. These are designated "non-carbonate hardness". The two forms of hardness combined make up general hardness (GH), also measured in degrees, which in this case vary from country to country - those used in this book are German, °dGH. 0-4 °dGH denotes (roughly) very soft, 4-8 °dGH soft, 8-12 °dGH medium hard, 12-18 °dGH hard, 18-30 °dGH very hard, and more than 30 °dGH extremely hard, water.

The pH value is closely connected with hardness, although they are totally separate concepts chemically. The pH value denotes the degree of acidity of the water. It is important to realize that pH is measured using a logarithmic decimal scale, so that water with a pH of 5 is 10 times as acid as pH 6, and 100 times as acid as pH 7. Because the components of carbonate hardness react very strongly with acids, in the aquarium mainly with carbonic acid, the concepts of hardness and pH are very much intertwined from an aquarium viewpoint. Water with a pH of 7 is designated neutral, water with a ph above 7 is termed alkaline, and that with a pH below 7 is acid. The extremes that (specialized) fishes can tolerate are an acid pH of 3.5 and an alkaline pH of 9.5.

The pH can fluctuate dramatically with the day-night rhythm, and this is often the reason why fishes become sick or die. The reason for this pH fluctuation is that at night plants do not use carbon dioxide as they are not engaged in photosynthesis, and in fact actually give off additional carbon dioxide via their respiration. In hard water this has little effect, as the carbonate hardness "cancels out" the carbon dioxide (the technical term for this is "buffering"). However, soft water has little or no buffering capacity (i.e. carbonate hardness) and this can result in pH surges that are life-threatening for the fishes.

There are three methods of avoiding this danger. Firstly an airstone can be used in the aquarium at night. Carbon dioxide is highly volatile and can thus easily be driven off from the water. Alternatively, humic acid can be added via peat filtration or as a liquid preparation, and this will also have a buffering effect, though this method can be used only for fishes that will tolerate acid water. Otherwise, for fish that don't like acidity, the water must be artificially hardened - method 3.

Hardness and pH should be monitored regularly.

Sexual somersaults

Vivarium keepers tend to be enthusiastic observers where their pets are concerned. Successful breeding and observation of the mating procedure are the high points of animal ownership. This is the ultimate proof, of course, that the person concerned has learnt to understand his pets and to make proper provision for their living requirements in captivity.

Dwarf clawed frogs adopt a rather unusual mating position, which they share with their South American cousins, the Surinam toads, and with the tropical clawed frog, *Silurana tropicalis*. First the sexually aroused male starts to call, often simultaneously propped up on his forelegs on the ground with his hind legs wide outspread. This calling, which sounds like a gentle clicking, apparently serves to advertise his territory and frighten away male conspecifics. When the male finds a female, he embraces her around the hips. Often the girl of his dreams is less than delighted at this approach and endeavours to be rid of her unwanted lover. But the latter doesn't give up that easily. He seeks to stimulate the female by rhythmic, pumping clasping. A further method of pacification and stimulation involves extending a hind-leg far forwards and rub-

Amplexus (mating embrace) in the dwarf clawed frog *Hymenochirus boettgeri*. The male is the dark-colored individual in the drawings.

bing the head of the female with the foot. If the female is actually ready to mate, i.e. she has ripe eggs in her belly, then these measures will generally bring her round to the male's way of thinking. And now the mating sequence begins. First of all the pair rest on the bottom of the aquarium. Then they both swim together vertically to the water's surface, take in air, allow themselves to sink down a little, and then perform a backward somersault, during which they contact the water's surface. The eggs and sperm are expelled at the highest point of this backward somersault. About 5-10 eggs are laid at each spawning pass, and the complete clutch comprises a maximum of about 200 eggs, which float at the surface and have a diameter of about 1.5 mm. They look rather like poppy seeds and have two poles, one light, one dark.

In order to breed you must, of course, have both sexes. So how do you distinguish the sexes in dwarf clawed frogs? In the first place the males are smaller and daintier. But this is not a guaranteed characteristic. However, males have well developed glands immediately behind their forelegs, absent in females. They look like small pimples and are easily visible with the naked eye, but unmistakable under a magnifying glass. In order to check for this feature, the relevant frog should be carefully caught out of the aquarium by hand. It will try to get away, kicking with its hind legs to free itself. If possible, hold it firmly by the hind legs, gently pressing them against the palm of the hand with the thumb. This will immobilize the frog and it can then be examined without any risk of harming it.

Dwarf clawed frogs often spawn spontaneously, especially if they are captive bred. If they don't, however, but the female's spawning tube is clearly visible, then mating can be triggered by an extensive program of water changes using cool water (about 16-18 °C), performed over a period of several days. After each water change the temperature should always return quickly to the normal 26-28 °C. This procedure will simulate a rainy period, such as triggers the spawning of dwarf clawed frogs in nature.

As already mentioned, the spawn floats at the surface. Because the parents will regard this as a welcome change of diet, they should be removed immediately after spawning. This is rather easier than moving the spawn, as the eggs are prone to stick to spoons, bowls, etc, and optimal development can be expected only if they are free-floating. Depending on water temperature, the larvae will begin to hatch after 2-3 days. They then hang on any available aquatic plants or the aquarium glasses for 5-6 days. During this period the larvae do not yet feed, instead relying on their yolk sacs for nourishment. Only when the larvae begin to swim free in the water (to do so they must first gulp in air) should you begin to feed them.

The tadpoles of dwarf clawed frogs are carnivores that feed on micro-organisms which they filter out of the water. If you have a source of the renowned Californian Artemia, then they can be fed with freshly hatched *Artemia* right from the start. *Artemia* nauplii from other sources are, however, too large. In such cases the only possible method of supplementary feeding is with infusorians. (See blue pages 44-45 for details of culturing Artemia nauplii and infusorians.) In any case, after at most a week *Artemia* nauplii can be offered. From now on growth will be rapid. After about 1-2 months (this depends on the food supply and water temperature) the tadpoles will metamorphose into tiny frogs. On completing this metamorphosis, young clawed frogs are about 1 cm long.

Pregnancy testing

The people of the western world always want to know as early as possible whether conception has taken place. The first scientifically accurate, and at the same time easy to administer, pregnancy test involved clawed frogs, specifically members of the genera *Xenopus* and *Silurana*. If the first morning urine of a pregnant woman is injected into the dorsal lymph sac of a sexually ripe female of these species, then the pregnancy hormone choriongonadoptrophin in the urine will cause the frog to lay eggs within at most 12 hours.

Even before this discovery, during the 1940s clawed frogs (in particular *Xenopus laevis*) were in demand as laboratory animals, used for innumerable researches into the fundamentals of neurophysiology and genetics. But this led to a veritable "run" on these creatures, such that laboratory breeding became increasingly important as the supply of wild specimens (by ship from Africa) was less than reliable. Plus our grandparents apparently already appreciated of the benefits of family planning.

Later on it was discovered that this type of test could also be conducted using native frogs, albeit not on females. The ripening of females of the central and western European frog species Rana temporaria is highly seasonal and possible during only a few weeks of the year. But males (if correctly treated) are almost always sexually ripe, and will evidence pregnancy by producing semen strings after a urine injection.

Nowadays, however, it is very unusual to find an aquarium full of clawed frogs in the gynecologist's waiting-room. But the fact that frogs react positively to human sex hormones continues to be put to good use by frog breeders all over the world, in cases where sexually-ripe individuals cannot otherwise be induced to spawn.

Only males of the European common frog (*Rana temporaria*) are suitable for pregnancy testing.

The african clawed frog, *Xenopus laevis*, has long aroused interest among humans. Xenopus means "strange foot". In Africa, mysterious powers have been ascribed to these frogs. Because of their sudden appearance in pools after the rains, they were thought to be rain-bringers, and many other myths and legends surround these amphibians. In Europe, however, scientists have taken a more pragmatic interest in these animals. Their morphological and developmental characteristics have been studied. Modern science has used them for cloning (i.e. to produce genetically identical individuals) and for other genetic research. Modern gene technology was developed using clawed frogs, and today the genetic make-up of the african clawed frog is among the best-known in the world.

This frog also entered the vivarium hobby at an early stage, inter alia because of its enormous temperature tolerance (it can be maintained at temperatures between 12 and 36 °C, although the optimum is about 22 °C). These frogs can even be kept in unheated aquaria without problems. The first reports of maintenance and breeding were published as early as 1905.

The african clawed frog has a vast distribution in Africa and is divided into five subspecies, in each case linked by intermediate forms. *X. Laevis laevis*, the nominate form (the term for the first subspecies described), inhabits the southern zone: South Africa, Namibia, eastern Botswana, Malawi, and Zimbabwe. This is the largest of all clawed frog forms. The dark gray back is usually speckled with fine black, but the coloration is variable and can also consist of large round spots. The belly is yellowish-white, either without markings or finely speckled. The call consists of long trills. The distribution of *X. l. poweri* adjoins

that of *X. l. laevis*: Zambia, western Botswana, and Angola (except for the northwest), southeastern Congo, and the Unzungwe Mountains in southwestern Tanzania. This frog too is rather large. It is dark olive-brown above, with 8-15 dark spots; the ventral coloration is as in *X. l. laevis*, but sometimes more densely speckled. The call is quite different, and can be described as a sonorous grah-grah-grah. Unlike the nominate form, i.e. *X. laevis laevis*, the inner side of the legs is often speckled. *X. l. sudanensis* is also notably widespread, and inhabits the central African Jos Plateau, eastern Nigeria, western and central Cameroon, and the Central African Republic. This form is similar to the preceding two, but smaller and generally with more prominent dorsal spots. The call is different too, supposedly consisting of irregular rattling trills (I have this only on hearsay, I have never heard it myself). *X. l. victorianus* inhabits Uganda, Tanzania, and Kenya. This form is relatively large, has a yellowish- to olive-green back, and, unlike the other subspecies, a rapid trilling call. *X. l. petersi* inhabits northwestern Angola, the Congo, and probably also Gabon. Its call has not yet been described, but it can be readily differentiated from other clawed frogs by its large ventral spots, larger than in any other subspecies.

The largest female of the nominate form collected to date measured 12.5 cm. It was found in a goldfish pond, where it had grown fat on a diet of ornamental fish! Males always remain smaller. The african clawed frog is totally adaptable and is found in pools and lagoons as well as rivers and lakes. Feral populations have colonized garden ponds and parks. In short, it has a finger in every pie, so to speak. Our aquarium strains are probably no longer pure-bred subspecies. If you are able to obtain wild-caught specimens, then you should avoid creating further cross-bred strains.

The normal form of the african clawed frog, *Xenopus laevis*, is only rarely kept in the aquarium. It is, however, one of the most important laboratory animals all over the world, and bred in millions.

The cultivated albino form of *Xenopus laevis* is regularly seen in the pet trade.

I have only once owned a strikingly colored *Xenopus laevis* like this. It was a female. Unfortunately it died as the result of an accident before I could breed it.

In 1864 the famous zoologist John Edward GRAY described *Silurana tropicalis*, a new, uncommon, species of frog from Africa, on the basis of a number of tadpoles and newly metamorphosed young frogs. In the tadpole stage this remarkable creature has two long barbels, no teeth, well-developed eyes, a ribbon of fin running round its body (similar to in an eel), and a second, short fin beneath its body. None of the fins has any supporting rays. GRAY was perfectly clear that it was a frog. The name of the new genus that he erected is composed of the Latin words silurus (= a type of catfish) and rana (= frog). He chose this name to denote the quite astonishing similarity to a catfish as bizarre tadpoles of this kind had never before been seen or described by anyone. This is the species which we today know as the ropical clawed frog.

Perhaps it is appropriate to digress slightly at this juncture and explain what a tadpole usually looks like. All tadpoles, except those of pipids, possess horny labial teeth arranged in bands. The tadpoles use these labial teeth (which are so characteristic in form and arrangement that they can be used to identify the species) to scrape off particles of food, which, depending on the species, consists of Aufwuchs (the name for the coating and algae and small organisms on rocks, wood, leaves, etc) or animal food.

As already mentioned, however, the tadpoles of pipid frogs do not have any labial teeth. We have already seen how the tadpoles of the dwarf clawed frogs are active hunters, which capture very small organisms swimming free in the water. The tadpoles of clawed frogs of the genera *Xenopus* and *Silurana*, and also their South American cousins, the small and medium-sized Surinam toads, have evolved as filter-feeders. In other words, they have adopted a way of life corresponding to that of small fishes that feed on plankton (by plankton is meant the totality of all organisms swimming free in water). In addition, the tadpoles of the genera *Xenopus* and *Silurana* also have long barbels that look exactly like the upper-lip barbels of certain catfishes (e.g. the glass catfishes, *Kryptopterus*).

In the wild these tadpoles swim free in the water, specifically in shoals. The similarity to fishes is truly remarkable.

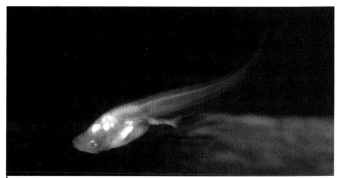
Tadpole of *Xenopus laevis*, the tropical clawed frog. The similarity to a catfish is amazing.

Just for comparison: an Indian glass catfish, *Kryptopterus minor*.

The tropical clawed frog

Having already encountered its tadpoles, let us now turn to the frog itself: *Silurana tropicalis*, the tropical clawed frog. The majority of clawed frog species have claws only on the three inside toes of each hind foot. A few species, however, including the tropical clawed frog, have evolved an additional horny claw on the so-called prehallux. This may perhaps indicate that these species perform migrations across land where such an additional claw would be of great use, similar to athletes' spikes.

The natural history of the tropical clawed frog has been described very vividly by RÖDEL (Herpetofauna of West Africa, vol. I: Amphibians of the West African Savannah. Editions Chimaira, Frankfurt am Main, 2000). He researched in great detail the Anura of the Camoé National Park, Ivory Coast, where he found the tropical clawed frog above all in pools in gallery forest (a type of forest found mainly along rivers). During the dry season the tropical clawed frog usually leaves these pools – of necessity, as they generally dry up. The dry season is generally spent in the bank zones of the rivers, where the frogs hide by day beneath stones or wood. They sometimes, however, supposedly survive the dry season by burying themselves in the bottom mud of their pools. As soon as the rainy season begins, the frogs migrate back to their forest pools, often occupying even the smallest bodies of water. RÖDEL reports that he regularly found them in the wash-bucket outside his hut! The adults are not particularly demanding as regards the water they live in. They are found in every type of pool, often even in muddy conditions. However, RÖDEL found tadpoles only in the larger forest pools, with dense underwater vegetation, that contained clear water even during the rainy season. This may signify that the tropical clawed frog also undertakes migrations to its spawning waters.

Tropical clawed frogs are highly recommended for aquarium maintenance, but unfortunately it is very difficult to obtain these frogs via the normal channels. I picked mine out of consignments of Böttger's dwarf clawed frog from Nigeria. These specimens were supposedly collected relatively close to Lagos.

Silurana tropicalis is one of the smallest clawed frog species, and, with a length of about 4 cm, grows little larger than the dwarf clawed frogs. It is not easy to differentiate the sexes in young specimens, but sexually mature males have so-called copulatory calluses on the inner side of their thumbs. Moreover the lobed abdominal processes (see photo) are more apparent in females than in males.

Tropical clawed frogs, *Silurana tropicalis*.

The tropical clawed frog

Silurana tropicalis can be highly variable in its markings.

The triggering of spawning in clawed frogs is the same as already described for dwarf clawed frogs. However, in the case of the african clawed frog (*Xenopus laevis*) the heavy artillery can be brought in. The water changes can be made using cooler water (14-16 °C). In addition, a regular "winter rest" at 10-12 °C is often very beneficial as regards breeding. This "winter rest" of the african clawed frog must take place in water. The best method is to place the frogs individually in suitably large, plastic containers in a refrigerator set to the correct temperature. The winter rest should last for 6-8 weeks. Feeding should cease two weeks before the planned winter rest, to avoid any problems caused by undigested food residues in the gastro-intestinal tract. Of course, the frogs should not be placed straight into such cool conditions but cooled down gradually over a period of weeks. In some areas it may be possible to achieve this by keeping them outside (e.g. on a balcony or patio). Suitable containers include large, escape-proof bowls or buckets, containing a few empty flowerpots as hiding-places. In temperate climates temperatures often continually drop to 10-15 °C in early autumn, and this will leave the frogs nicely conditioned for the refrigerator. They should not be fed during the winter rest.

After the winter rest, the frogs can be returned to normal room temperature in a very short time. It is advisable initially to fill the aquarium with cold water whose temperature matches that of the refrigerator, and then introduce the frogs immediately. The aquarium water temperature will generally rise to ambient within 24 hours. Breeding activity in the african clawed frog may commence at 15 °C, but the optimum temperature is 22 °C. It is not the case that the frogs will begin to spawn immediately after the winter rest – they cannot simply be "switched on" like a light and must be allowed a few days space. Plus, of course, they need plenty of nourishing food after their winter rest. They do not like spawning on an empty stomach!

In the african clawed frog too, the mating sequence is initiated by the calling of the male. Laboratory strains often apparently derive from South African specimens of the nominate form, as their call is usually described by breeders as a long-drawn-out trill. But it is always interesting to listen more closely. My first clawed frogs, which I acquired in 1983, had a quite different call, and sounded like the tapping of a hammer on a water pipe. Perhaps I had *X. laevis poweri*, but at that time I as yet knew nothing about all the different calls of *Xenopus* and for that reason paid little attention to such things. Females too are vocally endowed. Their call is a gentle short tick.

Courtship begins with the male going looking for a wife. Just like the dwarf clawed frogs, the african clawed frog clasps the female around her hips. If she is ready to mate, she immediately bends her legs. By contrast females that are not ready to mate keep their legs outstretched.

Unlike the dwarf clawed frogs, african clawed frogs do not perform a mating somersault. They swim around for a while in amplexus, spawning as they do so. The eggs are attached individually to plants or other objects, or expelled into the water. After spawning jelly surrounding the embryo swells up considerably. On the one hand this permits better attachment (e.g. where they have been laid among plants), while on the other it makes it more difficult for harmful micro-organisms to penetrate the gelatinous layer to the delicate embryo inside. A total of 500-1000 eggs can be expected from a single pair.

In the african clawed frog too, the parents are not averse

to a little caviar, hence they should be removed from the breeding aquarium (which should be about 40 x 40 x 40 cm in size) after spawning.

At 22 °C the larvae hatch after about 2-3 days. Again, they feed initially from the yolk sac, but once they become free-swimming (for this they must break surface and gulp air) it is up to the owner to provide these filter-feeders with the correct food. The main problem with this is that the tadpoles, unlike in the dwarf clawed frogs, filter-feed upon the tiniest particles of food. And, if they are to grow properly and thrive they need to be "up to their necks in food" as the saying goes.

In practice this food will consist of baker's yeast and stinging nettle powder. Baker's yeast can be bought cheaply at any supermarket, while you can make stinging nettle powder yourself by collecting as many young stinging nettle as possible, drying them, and finally pulverizing them. I use a small electric coffee grinder for this, but you can also use a food processor or liquidizer. The yeast and/or the stinging nettle powder are first of all put into suspension (mixed with water) and then placed in a very fine sieve. This sieve is then swirled around in the aquarium so that the "food solution" is dispersed. In order to keep the food moving as long as possible, you will need either to aerate (using large bubbles - under no circumstances using a fine diffuser as the tadpoles may swallow the tiny bubbles of air and die wretchedly as a result!) – or suspend a small powerhead (without filter attached) in the aquarium. The current should not be too strong. Because the water very rapidly becomes polluted by this type of feeding, a large water change must be performed every day, at the same time carefully siphoning all particles of dirt off the bottom. It is often suggested that small aquatic snails of various species should be used as scavengers but in my experience this rarely works. The snails are relatively

sensitive to poor water conditions, and often die off rapidly, causing additional pollution of the water.

All in all, rearing the tadpoles is thus rather time-consuming, and it is preferable to rear just a few dozen instead of attempting mass-production where you can easily lose them all.

Other options are available to anyone lucky enough to own a garden. It is possible to obtain very cheap plastic water tanks of about 60 liters capacity from builders merchants. Buy four or five of these, fill them with mains water, and place them in the garden in a sunny spot. To each batch of water add a quantity of a commercial horticultural fertilizer, at the rate recommended for watering plants. The result of this – from a water technology viewpoint – catastrophic over-fertilization will be an algal bloom. Ideally the water will become completely opaque grass-green. This "brew" is the ideal rearing medium for clawed frog tadpoles. Because the tadpoles, like the parents, are largely temperature-tolerant, they can usually be put outside for rearing from the middle of May to the end of July in temperate climates. If the water clarifies too much, they must be moved into the next container. An old algae-breeder's trick, in the event of insufficient algal growth, is to mix a few cc of urine into the water.

All very well in theory, but...... Sometimes the right sort of algae simply won't grow and you are left with thread or slime algae. The former represents a mortal danger for tadpoles, as they can become trapped in it and die miserably. The latter is unsuitable as tadpole food. It is a very good to experiment a little before you have a successful spawning.

The developmental period of the tadpoles is about 40

days at 22 °C; outdoors it is, of course, very much dependent on the weather.

If you attempting to rear outdoors, you must always make sure that the rearing container is absolutely escape-proof. Even in temperate climates there is a danger of these frogs becoming naturalized! The freshly-metamorphosed frogs, just like dwarf clawed frogs, can use their moist bellies as suckers and work their way up vertical glass surfaces. If it rains hard, then the tadpoles may be washed out of an overflowing container and thus escape into natural waters. This must be prevented at all costs, as introduced species can cause absolute devastation in the wild (see chapter "The clawed pest").

The breeding of the tropical clawed frog, *Silurana tropicalis*, follows a somewhat different pattern. An important reason why Silurana is regarded by most scientists as a distinct genus, rather than part of *Xenopus*, is that *Silurana*, just like the dwarf clawed frogs, mates with a backward somersault. In addition, the eggs of *Silurana* float at the water's surface.

However, the tadpoles are filter-feeders, just as in *Xenopus*, and rearing them is correspondingly more difficult. They develop more rapidly than those of *Xenopus laevis*, although they require rather higher temperatures, with 25 °C ideal. Oh, and adult *Silurana tropicalis*, which inhabit the tropics, can be stimulated to breed without a winter rest period. It has been found effective to raise the temperature to about 30 °C for breeding, feed heavily, and perform no water changes for 4-5 weeks.

Following this, perform several large (about 80% of tank volume) water changes, using cooler water (about 24 °C) over a period of several days, and then heat the water rapidly back to about 30 °C immediately after the water change. Spawning will generally take place at the end of this procedure.

As already mentioned, the development of the tadpoles is more rapid than in *Xenopus* and the metamorphosis takes place after only 25-30 days.

The tadpoles of *Silurana* are exceptionally sociable and are found together in shoals even when no enemy has upset them. The filter-feeding tadpoles of *Xenopus* and *Silurana* adopt a typical stance with the head inclined slightly downwards.

After metamorphosis young *Xenopus laevis* and *Silurana tropicalis* can be fed in the same way as their parents, except that the food particles must be correspondingly smaller.

Spawn of *Xenopus laevis*.

Infusoria

Artemia nauplii are often unsuitable as a first food for very small youngsters, as they are too large. In such cases it is necessary to fall back on the even smaller food organisms known as infusoria.

They are known as infusorians because the classic method of producing them is by making an infusion of hay. A handful of good quality hay (or bruised lettuce leaves) is placed in a large jar of perhaps 2 liters capacity which is then filled with aquarium water. After a short time the water becomes cloudy and begins to smell somewhat. The clouding and the beguiling perfume result from the massive proliferation of bacteria that use the hay as a source of food. Bacteria are no use as food as they are too small. But, after 3-4 days the water in the glass will become clear again and the stench also disappears. What has happened?

Through the glass it is possible to see tiny whitish streaks swimming, even with the naked eye: these are slipper animalcules (*Paramecium*), so-called because they look just like a comfortable old felt slipper. There are lots of other infusorians as well, whose existence is revealed under the microscope: *Vorticella*, amoebae (*Amoeba*), and various others. All these organisms feed on bacteria, which explains why the water in the infusion jar becomes clear again. It is the slipper animalcules that are the most important as food, however. Once the water is relatively clear, then the whole culture should be strained through a standard kitchen sieve into another container to remove the vegetable debris. The water and infusorians are then used as food in the rearing aquarium. It is important to make sure that the temperature of the infusorian water matches that of the aquarium. The easiest way to ensure this is to suspend the container of water in the tank for an hour, and then pour it in.

Culturing infusorians is not always problem-free. Sometimes the brew stinks for days on end, never becomes clear, and eventually turns black and putrid. In such cases the amount of hay was too great and too much oxygen was used as it decomposed – and without oxygen *Paramecium* & co. cannot survive. Often a very tough "crust" forms, composed of bacteria and yeasts, and must be removed if possible.

In order to avoid these imponderables, many aquarists use pure cultures of slipper animalcules. These cultures may not be anything like as productive, but they have the advantage of always being available if needed, and they don't smell. To start such a culture, rinse some used aquarium filter wool in a small basin of water. Tip the water, dirt and all, into a 1 liter clear wine bottle and add 1-2 drops of condensed milk using a pipette (pure cultures of *Paramecium* are fed on condensed milk at the rate of 1-2 drops per liter of water, re-dosing when the water becomes clear again.). It has proved effective to aerate very gently (one bubble per second) using an airline . Within a relatively short time you will see *Paramecium* developing. To harvest them, remove the airline and stuff some filter wool into the neck of the bottle, and fill the bottle to the brim with clean mains water so that there is about 4 cm of water in the neck of the bottle above the filter wool. A shortage of oxygen will develop fairly rapidly in the bottom of the bottle, and the *Paramecium* will instinctively head for the oxygen-rich zone at the surface. They will work their way through the filter wool and can then be collected, free of dirt, using a pipette.

Home-bred rotifers (Rotatoria) are also an excellent food for rearing. They too are fed with condensed milk. Unfortunately starter cultures are not available in the trade, so you will need to get one from a fish breeder.

Hatching Artemia

Artemia salina belongs to an ancient group of crustaceans, the so-called branchiopods (gill-feet). They are characterized by all species having adapted to periodic drying-up of their habitat by producing reproductive cysts, often termed eggs by aquarists. These "eggs" can survive in the bottom mud for weeks, months, even years of drought. Brine shrimps have adapted to a particularly saline habitat, although other branchiopods react rather badly to salt. Naturally, in their extreme habitat *Artemia* have no enemies and can proliferate massively – which is the basis of this small creature being used commercially as a fish food. The Artemia available in the trade originate mainly from the great salt lakes of the USA. Adult Artemia are about 1.5 cm long. While most other food organisms live in waters also inhabited by fishes, this is not the case with *Artemia*. Hence brine shrimp are never carriers of fish diseases, *Artemia* is an indispensable food during the acclimatization of stress-sensitive wild-caught fishes.

Artemia eggs can be purchased at any aquarium store. Salt water is required for hatching, and the salt concentration should be between 3 and 8% (= 30-80 g/l). The simplest way is to add 3 rounded tablespoonsful of salt to a liter of water if nauplii are required quickly because unexpected breeding has taken place. Some nauplii will always hatch at this salinity. But for an optimal hatch rate, if time permits, it is necessary to experiment a little with the salinity. Very often the salinity required for an optimal hatch rate will vary somewhat from batch to batch of eggs. At a temperature of 18-32 °C the nauplii hatch after 24-36 hours. The hatching time is temperature dependent. The culture should be left to stand for 48 hours before harvesting to obtain the maximum "crop".

It is easiest to use ordinary household cooking salt for culturing *Artemia*. But you must always make sure that the cooking salt doesn't contain added fluorine or iodine salts, as the *Artemia* will not tolerate these. Cooking salt sometimes has additives to make it flow freely – these will not harm the *Artemia*, but they will affect the strength of the salt solution. Often by the end of the packet there is more flow agent than salt left. I therefore recommend coarse crystal cooking salt, as sold for salt mills. This contains no flow agents and is easy to measure . The use of salt intended for marine aquaria is a luxury, and this rather expensive salt does produce an exceptional hatch rate. It should above all be used if you want to rear the *Artemia* and feed them to larger fishes.

To hatch a large quantity of *Artemia* eggs (up to about half a tablespoonful) you will need an airpump, airline, and an empty 1 liter bottle (clear wine bottles have proved very good) or a manufactured *Artemia* hatchery. For continuous feeding it is best to use two bottles (cheers!) or two hatcheries. It is all very easy, except that some people may find the bubbling of the bottles and the humming of the airpump irritating. If only small amounts of brine shrimp are required (for about 30-50 fry) then there is no noise. In that case you need only small (300 ml) jam jars filled with salt solution, and a knife-tip-full of eggs sprinkled on the surface. The surface tension of the water will keep the eggs at the surface until they hatch, so they will have plenty of oxygen.

Artemia nauplii always swim towards the light (this behavior is termed positively photo-active). To harvest them, turn off the aeration and tilt the container slightly towards a strong light source. The nauplii will then congregate on the side nearest the light, while the most recently hatched, still very young, *Artemia* congregate at the bottom of the container. Now they can simply be siphoned off with airline into an *Artemia* sieve. Don't forget to turn the aeration back on!

The clawed pest

The huge adaptability of the african clawed frog sometimes makes it a threat to other creatures, specifically when Xenopus laevis escaped from captivity and colonizes areas where it is not actually native.

The dangers attendant on such accidental introductions are legion. In the first place an "alien" organism may be in direct competition with an indigenous one, as unoccupied ecological niches are rare in nature. And the alien organism often proves the stronger, as its natural predators and other population controls are absent. The result is that the native species becomes scarce or goes extinct. For this reason the introduction of alien species is now, quite rightly, illegal over much of the world.

Another danger invariably posed by introduced species is that they may carry pathogens against which the native species have no immunity whatsoever. A good example of this is the fungal disease of crayfishes that was introduced to Europe by North American species and brought the European species to the verge of extinction.

So where does the african clawed frog stand in all this? Astonishing though it may seem, even in chilly Germany Xenopus laevis can be kept outdoors year round, and even bred. In 1949 Herman Kahmann published a very detailed article on this in the journal DATZ. There may to date be no permanent population of clawed frogs known in Germany, but it is possible they simply haven't been reported. Because of our senseless German conservation laws hardly anyone now goes "ponding". The danger of clawed frogs going feral here is, however, all too real, and hence it is essential that every owner of african clawed frogs should act responsibly and always make sure that

they don't escape into the wild. Elsewhere in Europe, clawed frogs have to date successfully colonized only parts of the UK, specifically the Isle of Wight (where they probably died out in the 1970s) and South Wales, where feral populations still exist. The largest populations are estimated at up to 1000 individuals! Further details can be found in Measley, G. J. & Tinsley, R. C., 1998: "Feral Xenopus laevis in South Wales." The Herpetological Journal 8: 23-27. So far the feral clawed frogs in South Wales appear not to have caused any harm.

Opinions are varied regarding the consequences of the introduction of the african clawed frog in California, Texas, and other states in the USA, as well as in Chile (Santiago). There are some very interesting web pages on the problem of "alien species", as introduced animals and plants are termed (the scientific terms neozoa (for animals) and neophyta (for plants) are also used) – e.g. http://www.issg.org - where much interesting information of worldwide origin has been assembled. Here too there is a warning about the african clawed frog. In California, however, where Xenopus laevis established itself in the 1960s and currently the state with the largest population outside Africa, the view is far more relaxed. Stomach contents analysis has shown that the tadpoles eaten by the clawed toads are almost exclusively those of their own species. Studies of the habitats of these frogs in California indicate that it colonizes mainly artificial ponds, where no native species are present. Perhaps in this case we have been lucky with the introduction of an alien species. Who knows?

Clawed frogs thus occupy above all artificial, rather sterile habitats, where they have established themselves outside their natural range. Researches into what they eat there have revealed an astonishing fact: at certain times the stomachs of the specimens examined contained mainly tadpoles of the same species!

Comparable researches have shown that the usual food of clawed frogs is chiefly large insects. In new, barren, habitats, however, there is sometimes a serious lack of food. It is true that clawed frogs aren't bothered by several weeks of fasting, but in the long term even *Xenopus* must eat something.

The survival strategy of these clawed frogs is to bring tadpoles into the world! At first glance that may seem illogical, but it isn't. *Xenopus* tadpoles are known to feed on micro-plankton, and this is hardly ever in short supply in newly constructed artificial ponds, as many owners of garden ponds learn to their sorrow. If you just consider that a single 6.5 cm female *Xenopus* can lay a good 1000 eggs at a time, and a 10.5 cm female 17,000, and that *Xenopus* generally spawn several times each breeding season, then it all becomes clear. The result of all this breeding activity is hundreds of thousands of *Xenopus* tadpoles, which convert micro-plankton (useless to adults) into valuable animal protein. This survival technique may appear morally reprehensible from a human viewpoint, but it is certainly effective.

Tadpoles of *Xenopus laevis* are sometimes used as food by their parents.

Threatened with extinction

Xenopus laevis has, however, become a genuine threat to its relatives in South Africa, which is home to, inter alia, the species *Xenopus gilli*, the Cape clawed frog, a small and particularly attractive member of the genus. It attains a length of only 5 cm. It is hypothesized that for a relatively short period (a few thousand years, maybe only a few hundred) the ranges of *Xenopus gilli* and *X. laevis* were isolated from one another and that some kind of barrier must have existed, insuperable for the african clawed frog

During this period *X. gilli* adapted to rather extreme environmental conditions and is now specialized for the very nutrient-poor near-coast waters in the South African coastal strip in the vicinity of Capetown. These waters have a pH of about 4 due to their humic acid content, and are also subject to occasional incursions of brackish water. These parameters, coupled with rather low temperatures (16-22 °C) are also required in captivity, and to date they have not been bred successfully, so the Cape clawed frog is rarely seen in the aquarium.

Xenopus gilli is not only smaller, but also less agile and predatory than its larger relative, *X. laevis*. Where both species occur together, they interbreed and produce hybrid populations. The period of time required for speciation in clawed frogs appears to be relatively short, and in this case the post-speciation period seems to have been insufficient to create barriers to hybridization. Similar instances are known among European frogs of the *Rana esculenta* complex and also among the livebearing toothcarps. Although its distribution appears to be less restricted than stated

Xenopus gilli, the Cape clawed frog.

above (new finds are regularly reported), the future still looks gloomy for the Cape clawed frog.

One subspecies of the african clawed frog is already extinct: *Xenopus laevis bunyoniensis*, described from Lake Bunyoni in Uganda. This was the form of african clawed frog with the longest legs of all. Nowadays only members of the subspecies *X. l. victorianus* are to be found in Lake Bunyoni. I know nothing about the reasons for this extinction. Perhaps tadpoles of *X. l. victorianus* gained entry to the lake along with introduced fishes, and subsequently outcompeted the endemic form. But it is also possible that *X. l. bunyoniensis* was overwhelmed by the species *X. wittei*, which has turned up in collections from the lake since the mid 1920s and has spread invasively since then. Unfortunately there is much uncertainty regarding the identification of old preserved material, preventing a precise reconstruction of events. So the fate of *X. l. bunyoniensis* remains a mystery.

So far we have discussed only a relatively small number of pipid species. There is a reason for this: it is always the same few species that are available in the trade and mentioned in the hobby literature. But there is a whole host of other species, all of them desirable as far as aquarium maintenance and breeding are concerned. With this regard, it is very interesting that there are probably a lot more species than are to date known to science. Time and again field studies suggest that the available data on the life history of a particular species are contradictory, and this makes it probable that in reality we are talking about several different species. In addition, numerous different species are confusingly similar in appearance and it is often very difficult to identify live specimens without knowledge of their origin. Moreover, because almost all the clawed frogs of the genus *Xenopus* can hybridize, it is very important to mate only individuals from the same locality and, if possible, to label them according to their origin or using some other additional identification (e.g. "imported from Gabon, 1987") so that aquarium populations can be kept pure-blooded.

Of course, the situation is not quite as problematical in the case of the dwarf clawed frogs, as various institutions worldwide are engaged in the breeding of numerous species. But things can change very rapidly, e.g. if the money dries up and the institution closes. Hence there follows a list of all the known species and their distributions. Of course, the distributions must be treated with circumspection as the actual range of many species has yet to be researched, and, moreover, it is not always clear to which species a particular researcher is referring. Here, then, is a list of all the species, while an identification key for the genera follows later on page 61.

Genus *Hymenochirus* BOULENGER, 1896 – dwarf clawed frogs

H. boettgeri boettgeri (TORNIER, 1896). Type locality: Ituri, near Wandesoma, German East Africa (now Tanzania). Known distribution to date: Nigeria, Congo basin to East Congo, western and southern Cameroon. About 3.5 cm.

H. b. camerunensis PERRET & MERTENS, 1957. Type locality: Foulassi, Cameroon. Known distribution to date: Cameroon (Foulassi, Ebelowa, Bouguma). About 3.5 cm.

H. boulengeri DE WITTE, 1930. Type locality: Uélé, northeastern Democratic Republic of the Congo. Not reported from further collections to date. About 3 cm.

H. curtipes NOBLE, 1924. Type locality: Zambia (lower Congo). Known distribution to date: lower Congo basin. About 3 cm.

H. feae BOULENGER, 1905. Type locality: Fernand-Vaz, French Congo. Known distribution to date: Democratic Republic of the Congo and Gabon.

Genus *Pseudhymenochirus* CHABANAUD, 1920
P. merlini CHABANAUD, 1920. Type locality: Conakry (Guinea). Known distribution to date: Guinea Bissau, Guinea, Sierra Leone.

Genus *Silurana* GRAY, 1864
S. epitropicalis FISCHBERG, SOLOMBELLI, & PICARD, 1982. Type locality: Kinshasa region (D. R. Congo). Known distribution to date: Lowland rainforest east and west of the Cameroon mountains to the eastern border of the D.R. Congo and to northern Angola. About 7 cm (males about 20% smaller).
Specimens from Kinshasa are uniform gray-brown, while those from other areas have a marbled back with small yellow, black, and olive spots. Call: whahawhahawha (about 5 "wha" per second).

S. tropicalis GRAY, 1864. Type locality: Lagos (Nigeria). Known distribution to date: Lowland rainforest in West Africa, from Nigeria to Senegal. About 5 cm. (Males

about 15% smaller.)
For coloration see photos in this book. Call: a deep rattle lasting several seconds: roaroar.....

Genus *Xenopus* Wagler, 1827 – clawed frogs
X. amieti DU PASQUIER, FISCHBERG, & GLOOR, 1980. Type locality: Mt. Manengouba (Cameroon). Known distribution to date: Cameroon (west, highlands above 1200 meters). About 5.5 cm (males about 25% smaller). The back is dark gray-brown, a transverse band is often present, a few irregular dark spots on the back and legs. Call: short, high-pitched, metallic clicks: cri, cri (about 2/sec).

X. andrei LOUMANT, 1983. Type locality: Longyi (close to Kribi, Cameroon). Known distribution to date: Cameroon (north and lowlands). About 4 cm (males about 5-10% smaller). Indistinguishable from the very similar X. fraseri in coloration, the lower eyelid covers only about half the eye (three quarters in X. fraseri). Call: short trill (about 0.5 secs.): riing, riing.
X. borealis PARKER, 1936. Type locality: Marsabit (Kenya). Known distribution to date: Kenya (normally above 1500 meters, lower only at Marsabit). About 7.5 cm (males about 20% smaller:
Dark brown to steel-blue, with 30-40 irregular black spots, closer together on the posterior body and hindlimbs. Call: similar to a bouncing table-tennis ball: tack, tack – usually 2/sec., occasionally increasing to up to 12/sec.
X. boumbaensis LOUMONT, 1983. Type locality: Mawa, in the Boumba valley, Cameroon. Known distribution to date: known only from the Boumba valley. About 3.5% (males 25-30% smaller).
Yellowish olive, with elongate dark spots behind and between the eyes, numerous dark small spots on the back and hindlimbs.

Call: 1-2 metallic impulses/sec.: crick, crick.
X. clivii PERACCA, 1898. Type locality: Saganeiti and Adi Caié (Eritrea). Known distribution to date: Ethiopia, Eritrea, above 1500 meters altitude. About 7 cm (males 25% smaller).
Grey-brown with 15-30 irregular dark spots, hindlimbs with elongate spots. The nuptial coloration on male forelegs extend to the chest, a feature not seen in any other Xenopus species. Call: a rolling quack, once/sec.: qua, qua.
X. fraseri BOULENGER, 1905. Type locality: West Africa (no further details). Known distribution to date: Cameroon (south) and Gabon (north). About 4.5 cm (males 20-25% smaller).
Gray-brow, occasionally with a transverse band behind the eyes. Posterior body and hindlimbs with vermiculated markings. Call: long-drawn-out trills: iii-iiing, iii-iiing, with an impulse rate of 150/sec.
X. gilli ROSE & HEWITT, 1925. Type locality: Near Capetown (South Africa). Known distribution to date: South Africa (Cape region). About 5.5 cm (males about 30% smaller). For coloration see illustration in this book. Call: short trills: vrii, vrii, vrii, 1-3 calls/sec.
X. laevis laevis (DAUDIN, 1803). Type locality: South Africa ("Cape Colony"). Known distribution to date: Namibia, South Africa, Botswana (east), Zimbabwe, Malawi. About 11 cm (males about 25% smaller).
For coloration and calls of the various subspecies see chapter "The african clawed frog".
X. l. bunyoniensis LOVERIDGE, 1932. Type locality: Lake Bunonyi, Uganda. Known distribution to date: probably extinct. About 6 cm.
X. l. petersi DU BOCAGE, 1895. Type locality: Dondo (Angola). Known distribution to date: Angola (northwest), Congo (west). About 6.5% (males some 25% smaller).
X. l. poweri HEWITT, 1927. Type locality: Victoria Falls

The Victoria Falls in Zambia. The type material of *Xenopus laevis* poweri was collected in this area.

(Zambia). Known distribution to date: Namibia (north), Angola (except northwest), Botswana (Okavango), Zambia, D. R. Congo (southeast), Tanzania (southwest Unzunwe Mountains). About 6.5 cm (males some 20% smaller).

X. l. sudanensis PERRET, 1966. Type locality: Ngaoundéré (Cameroon). Known distribution to date: Central African Republic, Nigeria (east), Cameroon (west and central highlands). About 6 cm (males 20% smaller).

X. l. victorianus AHL, 1924. Type locality: Busisi, Lake Victoria (Tanzania). Known distribution to date: Uganda and bordering Sudan, Tanzania (north), Kenya (southwest), Burundi, Ruanda, D. R. Congo (east). About 6.5 cm (males 25% smaller).

X. largeni TINSLEY, 1995. Type locality: Sidamo province (southern Ethiopia). Known distribution to date: the Bale Mountains in southern Ethiopia at an altitude of around 2600 meters. About 5.5 cm (males 30% smaller). Uniform unspotted brown. Call: trills of 0.5 sec. duration, whriiing, whriiing.

In the hobby this species is known under the working name (cheironym, a scientifically meaningless name sometimes used before a species is scientifically described, where some form of identifier is required) X. "ethiopii".

X. longipes LOUMONT & KOBEL, 1991. Type locality: Lake Oku, Cameroon. Known distribution to date: only from the type locality. About 3.5 cm (males some 15% smaller).

Vivid caramel or brown, heavily sprinkled speckled or marbled, also with larger spots. Belly and throat likewise heavily speckled, often almost black on a gray to bright orange background. Call unknown.

The importation of this pretty little species would be highly desirable.

X. muelleri (PETERS, 1844). Type locality: Tete (Mozambique). Known distribution to date: reported from a huge distribution – Burkhina Faso, Ivory Coast, Ghana, Benin, Nigeria, Cameroon, Congo, Gabon, Angola, Chad, D. R. Congo, the Central African Republic, Sudan (in the south), Ethiopia, Uganda, Kenya, Tanzania, Zanzibar, Malawi, Zambia, Zimbabwe, Mozambique, Botswana, Swaziland, South Africa, Namibia. The species is divided into an eastern and a western form, distinguished mainly by their parasite faunas and their calls. Eastern form about 7 cm, western form about 8% (males 20% smaller).

Olive to gray-brown with 5-8 large dark spots that may fade with age. Call: the species can produce two different calls. One is reminiscent of a spoon tapping on a pan: tick-tick-tick (4-8/sec.). The other is more complex: trra, trra (2/sec.). In the western form the males are inclined to use the first call only as a mating call, and it is slower than in the eastern form; on the other hand, the second call, when used, is shorter. The systematic status of the two forms remains unclear.

X. pygmaeus LOUMONT, 1986. Type locality: Bouchia (Central African Republic). Known distribution to date: Central African Republic, D. R. Congo (northeast). About 3.5 cm (males 5-10% smaller).

Gray with a reddish cast, transverse bands often split into two longish bands, posterior body marbled. Call: long rattling trills: cracrracrocra.......

X. ruwenzoriensis TYMOWSKA & FISCHBERG, 1973. Type locality: Bundibugyo, Semliki valley, Uganda. Known distribution to date: known only from the Semliki valley. About 5.5 cm (males 20-25% smaller).

Coloration similar to *X. pygmaeus*, but, unlike that species, *X. ruwenzoriensis* has the underside of the legs spotted. Call: short, high-pitched, metallic trills: cri, cri (about 2/sec.).

X. vestitus LAURENT, 1972. Type locality: Rutshuru (D. R. Congo). Known distribution to date: Ruanda, Uganda, adjoining areas of the D. R. Congo (in the Virguna volcano region). About 5 cm (males 20% smaller).

Coloration very characteristic: a marbled pattern of silver and bronze shades overlaying a brown background. The head is lighter and separated from the rest of the body by a transverse band. Call: trills with a 0.5 sec. duration: triing, triing.

X. wittei TINSLEY, HOBEL & FISCHBERG, 1979. Type locality: Chelima Forest (southwest Uganda). Known distribution to date: Ruanda, Uganda, adjoining areas of the D. R. Congo (in the Virguna volcano region). About 5 cm (males 20% smaller). Uniform unspotted brown. Call: long ringing calls: trrrirrrirrri.......

The last two species listed are distinguished by the size of the eye, the call, and the coloration.

Sizes given are always average length attained, measured from the tip of the snout to the anus. Some individuals may grow larger, especially given optimal living conditions in the aquarium. Moreover females are essentially larger and heavier than males.

It is not easy to identify pipid species in life, especially if you don't have the opportunity to see different species together for comparison. This problem is perhaps not unconnected with the fact that there are so many species and so little information on them in the hobby literature. Also, the pet trade generally doesn't bother to identify the different species. Hence, as a rule, all *Hymenochirus* and *Pseudhymenochirus* are sold simply as "dwarf clawed frogs", and all *Xenopus* and *Silurana* as "Xenopus laevis".

The determination of the species of clawed frogs is often difficult. This specimen was imported with *Silurana tropicalis*.

Xenopus largeni

Xenopus muelleri

Xenopus laevis poweri

Xenopus laevis sudanensis

The world of the senses

The clawed frogs of the genus *Silurana* and *Xenopus* are so distinctive that even someone who has never before seen such a frog will recognize them as clawed frogs.

Their first striking feature is that the eyes are not positioned laterally on the head but look upwards. This is typical of all clawed frogs; and, moreover, some otherwise similar species can be differentiated by the size of the eyes and the distance between them. An example is the two species found in the Virunga volcano region, *X. ruwenzoriensis* and *X. boumbaensis*. In the former the eyes are larger and appreciably more up-turned.

The sense of sight plays only a subordinate role among clawed frogs. Even individuals that have lost their eyes through disease or injury behave fairly normally and can manoeuvre and capture prey as skillfully as before. However, the position of the eyes is certainly no accident. Clawed frogs are very fond of floating at the water's surface with all four limbs outspread, and their eyes permit them to peer above the surface as well.

Many species have a tentacle immediately below the eye, and this is perhaps used for chemical sensing, like the barbels in many fishes. These tentacles are absent in *Xenopus gilli* and *X. largeni*. The length of these tentacles in adult frogs is again species-specific.
X. muelleri has the longest tentacles, but they are also long in *X. andrei*, *X. clivii*, *X. fraseri*, and *X. pygmaeus*.

A further peculiarity of the clawed frogs is their lateral-line organs, which look rather like the rough-stitched scars of Frankenstein's monster! These lateral-line organs are complex sensory organs, not unlike the lateral line system in fishes. They perform numerous functions, and are sensitive to the slightest variations in water pressure. Thus pipids locate their prey with the help of the lateral-line organs, orient themselves spatially, detect the approach of larger (and potentially dangerous) animals, etc. The number and arrangement of the groups of sensory cells of the lateral-line organs is species-specific and hence can be used to determine the species.

In the dwarf clawed frogs (except *Pseudhymenochirus*, which is to be regarded as a primitive *Hymenochirus*) and some Surinam toads the lateral-line organs are hidden beneath the skin and not externally visible. The two groups are rather closely related and thus represent a nice example to support the theory of continental drift.

Xenopus muelleri

The surface of the earth consists of raft-like plates floating on the liquid core. Where two plates collide, one slides under edge of the other; where plates drift apart, magma wells up and solidifies. Both cases produce earthquake zones and volcanic activity. The continents we know today were not always thus: South America, Africa, Madagascar, India, and part of Indonesia once formed a single vast land mass, the ancient continent of Gondwana. In consequence, some types of animal that evolved when these land masses were still connected are today found in totally different parts of the world – the dwarf clawed frogs and the Surinam toads are an example.

Fossil finds of *Xenopus* in South America indicate that the two main groups of pipids – the clawed frogs on the one hand and the dwarf clawed frogs and Surinam toads on the other – had already evolved before South America and Africa separated.

Xenopus boumbaensis

Xenopus ruwenzoriensis

Xenopus wittei

Given the framework of anatomical knowledge provided by the previous chapter, you should now be able to use what is practically the only identification key for clawed frogs in existence. Together with the information in the chapter, "Untold diversity", it originates from the work by H. R. Kobel, C. Loumont, and R. C. Tinsley, "The extant species", which the authors presented at a symposium in London. It can be found in the published proceedings of the symposium, "The biology of *Xenopus*" (edited by R. C. Tinsley & H. R. Kobel), a volume in the series Symposia of the Zoological Society of London (No. 68, 1996).

To clarify some of the characters mentioned in the key, the inner sides of the hind feet of three clawed frogs are shown here: in each case the arrow indicates the diagnostic prehallux, which may bear a claw in

Silurana tropicalis

Xenopus muelleri

Xenopus laevis

some clawed frogs, for example *Silurana tropicalis*. The next drawing shows the head of two clawed frogs in profile. The lateral-line organ, the differing forms of the lower eyelid, and the subocular tentacle can be seen very clearly. Finally, three more drawings, of newly-metamorphosed frogs, are presented: in these the characteristic patterns (e.g. the transverse band in *X. muelleri*), and the subocular tentacle can again be seen very clearly. These drawings are taken from the work of J. Arnoult & M. Lamotte (1968), Les Pipidae de l'Ouest africain et du Cameroun. Bulletin de l'I.F.A.N., Tome III, Serié A., no.1., as are the excellent drawings of the tadpoles of a number of clawed frogs earlier in this book.

So, I hope you will now feel equipped, if the occasion arises, to identify a clawed frog using the identification keys, even without a prior course in biology – or at least to get close to an identification, itself no mean achievement.

Xenopus fraseri

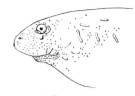

Silurana tropicalis

Xenopus fraseri

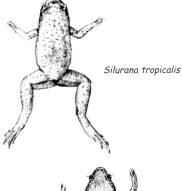

Silurana tropicalis

Xenopus muelleri

Key to identification

Identification key for dwarf clawed frogs

Lower eyelid motile;   externally-visible lateral-line organ.................................***Pseudhymenochirus merlini***
Lower eyelid fixed; no externally visible lateral-line organ .... ***Hymenochirus***

A. Sides of body covered in tubercles; head broad; body oval, elongate; dorsal surface plain-colored.

1. Webbing of hands and feet maximally developed, extending almost to the tips of the fingers and toes except for the inside edge of the 3rd toe where 1.5 phalanges are free of webbing; webbing highly pigmented, glandulous; size large: male 42 mm, female 46 mm. Former French Congo.........................***H. feae***

2. Webbing less developed, mainly on the hands where 1.5-2 phalanges remain unwebbed on the 3rd finger.. ***H. boettgeri***

a. a. Distance between eye and nostril (2.3-3 mm) always greater than eye diameter; head broad, eye diameter at least 37.6% of interocular space; pedal webbing moderately developed, inside edge of 3rd toe (the longest) free of webbing for 1.5-2 phalanges, webbing finely pigmented with black, creating a dark effect; size fairly large: males 32-35.5 mm, females 35-40.5 mm. From Cameroon, to the Ituri .... ***H. boettgeri boettgeri***
b. b. Distance between eye and nostril (1.8-2.3 mm) equal to or slightly greater than eye diameter; head narrower, eye diameter at least 44.2% of interocular space; pedal webbing well developed, almost to the extent seen in feae, inside edge of 3rd toe free of webbing for 1.5-1.75 phalanges; webbing clear with little pigmentation; size fairly small: males 28-31 mm,

females 30-35 mm. South-east Cameroon and Congo-basin. .... ***H. boettgeri camerunensis***

B. Sides of body homogenous, without any differentiated warts; head narrow; body pear-shaped; dorsal surface often spotted

1. 1. Tibia contained 2.5 – 2.75 times in snout-anus distance; tibio-tarsal articulation extending to the eye or a little beyond; size 27 mm. Uélé, north-east Congo .... ***H. boulengeri***

2. 2. Tibia contained 2.75-3 times in snout-anus distance; tibio-tarsal articulation extending only to the shoulder or a little beyond; size small: 24-28 mm. Lower Congo .... ***H. curtipes***

Identification key for clawed frogs

1. Three claws on hind foot (prehallux without claw)..........2
- Four claws on hind foot (prehallux with claw)...................8

2. Prehallux well-developed, conical......................................3
- Prehallux poorly developed or not visible..........................4

3. Subocular tentacle longer than half eye diameter; dorsum greenish brown, a few large round spots. Upper Volta to southern Sudan.................***X. muelleri*** (west)
East Africa, from southeast Kenya to South Africa ....***X. muelleri*** (east)

- Subocular tentacle at most half as long as eye diameter. Dorsum blue-gray with numerous elongate spots. Kenya..***X. borealis***

4. Subocular tentacle absent or at most visible as a small prominence. Prehallux not visible...5
- Subocular tentacle present. Prehallux visible....................6

5. Lower eyelid covering a third or less of eye. Ethiopia..***X. largeni***
 - Lower eyelid covering half of eye. South Africa (Cape region and coast to Cape Agulhas).....................***X. gilli***

6. Hind legs (measured from anus to 5th toe) 15-20% longer than body (measured from tip of snout to anus). 5th toe longer than tibia ....***X. laevis*** (for differentiation of subspecies see chapter, "The african clawed frog".)
 - Hind legs as long as or at most 5% longer than body. 5th toe as long as tibia...7

7. Color of head, dorsum, and limbs uniform olive-brown to chocolate-colored, no black spots........................***X. wittei***
 - Dorsum and limbs irregularly marbled light silvery-golden to bronze. Head lighter than rest of body. ....***X. vestitus***

8. Cloacal lobes joined together posteriorly. Lower eyelid covering less than a third of eye................................9
 - Cloacal lobes not joined. Lower eyelid covers less than half of eye...10

9. Size of nucleus of red corpuscles appreciably smaller than in *X. laevis*. West of the Cross River (Nigeria) to Senegal ....***Silurana tropicalis***
 - Size of nucleus of red corpuscles as in *X. laevis*. From the Cameroon mountains to the eastern border of the Democratic Republic of Congo, and south to northern Angola ....***S. epitropicalis*** (Without knowledge of their origin and laboratory equipment the two Silurana species can be told apart only by their calls.)

10. 5th toe longer than tibia..11
 - 5th toe about as long as tibia

....***Xenopus-fraseri-*group** (This group contains *X. fraseri, X. pygmaeus, X. amieti, x. andrei, X. boumbaensis*, and *X. ruwenzoriensis*. Without knowledge of their origin and laboratory equipment private owners can tell them apart only by their calls. See species description under "Untold diversity".)

11. Eyelid covering three quarters of eye; lateral-line organ with 12-16 groups of pores around the eye. Eritrea and Ethiopia ....***X. clivii***
 - Eyelid covering a third of eye; lateral-line organ with 7-13 groups of pores around the eye. Lake Oku in Cameroon...***X. longipes***

With this rather "dry" chapter we leave the fascinating world of the clawed frogs of Africa. The remaining pages are devoted to the pipids of the New World, the legendary Surinam toads of the genus *Pipa*.

The Surinam toads have attained nothing like as much significance for research or popularity in the aquarium hobby as have the dwarf clawed frogs and clawed frogs. Only rarely, and then only with a lot of luck and at rather a high price, does the opportunity arise to buy one of the seven species involved. In more than 25 years of intensive aquarium and terrarium activity, I myself have encountered only two species, and I have kept only one of them (*Pipa parva*) for a while. Anyone who expects regular flashes of temperament from the South Americans will find these pipids something of a disappointment. The majority of the Surinam toads (*Pipa*) are exceptionally phlegmatic creatures compared to their African cousins. The only exception is the dwarf Surinam toad (*Pipa parva*), but more of that anon.

First a brief summary of the known species:
Genus *Pipa* - Surinam toads
Pipa arrabali: northern South America and Panama. About 8 cm.
P. aspera: Venezuela (southeast), Guyana, Surinam, Brazil (Amazonas and Pará states). About 6 cm.
P. carvalhoi: Brazil (Pernambuco, Ceará, Espirito Santo, Bahia, Minas Gerais, Paraiba states). About 6 cm.
P. myersi: Panama (Darien province: Rio Chucunaque plain), Colombia (Rio Zulia). About 6 cm.
P. parva: Colombia (northeast), Venezuela (northwest). About 3 cm.
P. pipa: Bolivia, Colombia, Guyana, Surinam, Peru, Ecuador, Brazil, Trinidad. About 20 cm.
P. snethlagae: Brazil (Pará state). About 20 cm.

Unfortunately, as already mentioned, as far as I know to date only three species have been kept at all regularly and there are detailed breeding reports for only two of them: *Pipa pipa* and *P. carvalhoi*. There are not even usable photos of the other species. But, in case these creatures should become available, here is a brief description. Because of their warty skin, *Pipa arrabali* and *P. aspera* look rather like overgrown dwarf clawed frogs. *P. arrabali* is matt brown to ochre yellow on the back, with the dark warts standing out like dots. The belly is orange-brown dotted with dark brown. *P. aspera* is rather red-brown on the back; the belly is spotted dark brown, the throat region uniform dark brown. *P. myersi* is more like *P. carvalhoi*, i.e. relatively smooth. The back is gray-brown with dark spots (only occasionally marbled in *P. carvalhoi*), the belly is gray with ochre-colored spots (gray, often sprinkled with darker color, in *P. carvalhoi*). Finally, *P. snethlagae* is very similar to the large Surinam toad, but can be distinguished from the latter by its coloration, specifically the belly markings. In *P. pipa* the belly is characteristically covered with light criss-cross markings on a dark ochre-gray background; this pattern is absent in *P. snethlagae*. In *P. snethlagae* a dark streak runs from the posterior edge of the eye to the corner of the mouth, but is absent in *P. pipa*.

Of course, the Surinam toads are primarily distinguished from one another by anatomical characters, for example, leg length, head width, the form and presence/absence of the inner prehallux, and, above all, by the degree of development of the characteristic fingertips. In addition to the senses already discussed for the dwarf clawed frogs, the Surinam toads have very sensitive,

The large Surinam toad

The large Surinam toad, *Pipa pipa*, is certainly no beauty. But many people with an interest in nature will want to see its fascinating brood care for themselves.

several times forked, fingertips, that serve as highly sensitive organs of touch. This is probably a special adaptation to the often murky native waters of these pipids. I will not discuss the remaining anatomical differences further here, as they are difficult to put into words and for this reason of little use for identifying live specimens.

The first detailed report on the large Surinam toad (*Pipa pipa*) reached naturalists as long ago as 1719, in the second edition of the world-renowned book "Metamorphosen" (Metamorphoses) by Maria Sibylle Merian. This extraordinary lady from Frankfurt published a detailed engraving of a female with "ripe" young. The news that live young were born from the back of the road caused incredulous astonishment. In fact Merian had misunderstood how the eggs came to be in the back of the mother. Further misapprehensions were to follow. Thus, in 1764-65, FERMIN asserted that the female laid her eggs on land and then rolled on them until they remained stuck to her back; only then were they fertilized. Pure fantasy, as we now know. But in fact the truth was not discovered until 1960, almost 250 years after Merian's publication. This is the more astonishing in that Surinam toads are regarded as a delicacy by the natives and were less than rare in captivity. The species was bred in London (more specifically in the London Society's garden, now London Zoo) as early as 1896. A female was found to have eggs on her back, and her spawning tube was enlarged like a balloon. A real nuisance, that Surinam toads prefer to mate at night. As a result the actual process was not observed, but speculation was rife. The hypothesis was put forward that the female extended her spawning tube so far that she could place the eggs on her back herself. This idea also proved false. In actuality, Surinam toads employ much the same procedure as their small cousins from Africa, the dwarf clawed frogs: a backward somersault. Although in practice the eggs are not scattered on the water's surface as in *Hymenochirus*, but expelled during the downward movement. In fact the enlarged, inflated spawning tube of the female ensures that the eggs land on her back – but nothing more. During the downward movement, the male raises his body but without relaxing his grip around her hips. As the eggs appear, the male makes circular movements with his feet, perhaps the better to distribute his semen. Then he presses the eggs firmly into place with his belly. At this point the eggs are rather far back, on the end of the female's body. The male pushes them further forward with his hind feet, so that subsequent eggs have room on her back.

When the spawning is completed, the male relaxes his embrace. His job is done, and he now goes about his own private business. The spawn is still clearly visible on the back of the female, but in the course of the following eight days the eggs sink completely into the skin of the female's back, where the entire development to fully-formed young frogs takes place. This lasts (the process is temperature-dependent, but appears also to vary with the individual) 2.5-3.5 months (105-145 days). For several days before the juveniles are released from the back, they often protrude from the dorsal Surinam and even feed during this period! Unlike their African cousins, which we have found to be very fond of their own caviar and tadpoles, maternal Pipa pipa are not cannibals! In view of the high value of each specimen, breeders invariably isolate "pregnant" females. But in such cases it has been observed that the females even spit out any young that are accidentally taken into their mouths. The rearing of large Surinam toads is the easiest among all the pipids.

The large Surinam toad has one drawback: it grows rather large (in the case of females, you must reckon on a good 20 cm) and has a corresponding space requirement. An aquarium for large Surinam toads should be no smaller than 120 x 60 x 60 cm. Moreover *Pipa pipa* are rather pricey, so that putting together a breeding group is rather expensive.

But, as if Mother Nature was aware of these little problems, she has also provided us with *Pipa carvalhoi*, the Surinam toad for the man in the street, so to speak. This species grows to only about 6 cm long, and hence can readily be kept in a small group (2 males, 2 females) in the 60 x 30 x 30 aquaria readily available in the trade.

As in all pipids, the males remain smaller than the females and can call – an ability denied the females. The call has been described as a long-drawn-out trill, becoming increasingly more rapid and culminating in a humming sound. It is said of Pipa pipa that in well-fed individuals (beware, these animals easily become obese and are then no further use for breeding) the cloaca is thicker and rounder in females and its opening points upwards at an angle. In males the opening points downwards. Moreover in males the arms are thicker. Water chemistry is unimportant for breeding.

The spawning behavior of *Pipa carvalhoi* is as in *Pipa pipa*, although after spawning everything proceeds more rapidly. The eggs sink completely into the back of the female after only 24 hours. In practice this is a great advantage, as the eggs are of the large Surinam toad are exposed to numerous dangers during the long developmental process and this often results in serious losses, for example to snails (which eat the eggs), or through shedding of the egg if the female is frightened.

The young of *Pipa carvalhoi* begin to hatch after only 14 days, but in this case it is not fully-formed young frogs that leave the back of the female, but tadpoles about 12 mm long (3 mm body and 9 mm tail). Their appearance is highly reminiscent of that of clawed frog tadpoles, except that they have no barbels. They too are open-water filter-feeders, although they are capable of taking significantly larger food particles than *Xenopus* tadpoles. This makes rearing them appreciably easier; they can manage powdered dried food as sold for young aquarium fishes. The tadpoles take about six weeks to develop into frogs. When breeding Surinam toads, make sure that the water's surface is not overgrown with floating plants. The tadpoles of all pipids must break surface after hatching in order to become buoyant. This can sometimes be prevented by the presence of too many plants and lead to annoying losses.

Pipa carvalhoi

The small Surinam toad

When, some time ago, I saw my first small Surinam toad *Pipa parva*, I thought: "Oh yes, now they are breeding Hymeno-chirus in Venezuela." Only on closer examination did I realize that these little creatures had no black claws on their hind feet, but did instead have the forking of the fingertips typical of Surinam toads. They were indeed Surinam toads. This, the smallest of all the species, is imported from the Lake Maracaibo area. Its similarity to the dwarf clawed frogs is truly amazing, and its care does not differ at all from that of its African relatives. Because of the relative rarity of these animals, they should, at least initially, be kept in a species tank and not in a community aquarium with fishes. To date no breeding reports have been published for these amusing dwarfs. Their tadpoles (in this species too the juveniles leave their mother's back at the tad-pole stage) are noted for their very flat snouts. It is to be hoped that as many aquarists as possible will decide to keep the-se charming little animals, so that hopefully, in fu ture, they will become permanently availa-ble as captive-bred stock.

Pipa parva

Eclipse™ Aquarium System

ADVANCED TECHNOLOGY, SUPERIOR PERFORMANCE, UNLIMITED VERSATILITY...

Superior BIO-Wheel Filtration
Silent, high capacity 3-stage efficiency. BIO-Wheel and Eclipse Filter Cartridge unmatched by all other types of aquarium filtration.

Superior Illumination
Colour-enhancing fluorescent lighting. Far better that heat-producing incandescent bulbs. Plants thrive and colours of fish and plants come alive!

Superior Convenience
Easy set-up, easy operation. Polymer wool and carbon all-in-one filter cartridge changes in seconds, whilst the BIO-Wheel never needs replacing.

Superior View
Injection-molded acrylic aquarium provides a panoramic 360 degrees of prime viewing area for maximum enjoyment. Available as *Eclipse System 3* and *Eclipse Systems 6*.

Eclipse Explorer
Employs the same sophisticated BIO-Wheel filtration technology as the larger Eclipse Systems. Available in 4 additional fun colours, incorporating a textured skylight to maximise surrounding light.

Explorer = 7.5 litres   System 3 = 11 litres   Sytem6 = 22.5 litres

ALL AQUALOG TITLES & THE ABOVE PRODUCTS ARE DISTRIBUTED IN THE UK BY:

Specialists in Aquarium & Pet Technology

Belton Road West ~ Loughborough
Leicestershire ~ LE11 5TR
Tel: 01509 610310 ~ Fax: 01509 610304
E-mail: info@underworldproducts.co.uk
Web Site: www.underworldproducts.co.uk

Textbooks - detailed guides to maintenance and breeding

Most advisories include a beautiful poster!

■ Detailed guidance on maintenance and breeding, tricks and tips from experienced specialists

■ Many volumes include a decorative color poster (85 x 60 cm, also available separately)

■ Available in German and English editions

Shrimps, Crayfish and Crabs in the Freshwater Aquarium
(U. Werner)

We present the most beautiful freshwater crustaceans. Small and large species that can be kept alone or with fishes – but which? The answer, and much more, in this interesting and engrossing guide.

(64 pages)
ISBN 3-936027-08-0
Item no. AS010-E

Decorative Aquaria The Beginner´s tank
(U. Glaser sen.)

For the first time a detailed guide to setting up a perfect, beautiful, aquarium for the novice. Expert advice on avoiding beginners´ mistakes. Tank layout, plant and fish populations; all illustrated, and described in detailed but easy-to-understand terms.

(48 pages + poster)
ISBN 3-931702-38-3
Item no. AS011-E

The Natural Garden Pond
(P. D. Sicka)

A garden pond that imitates nature is a refuge for innumerable endangered animals and plants. Numerous examples and splendid photos demonstrate clearly how to create a dream of a miniature biotope in your own garden.

Available in German only.

(48 pages)
ISBN 3-931702-90-1
Artikel-Nr. AS021-D

The most beautiful L-numbers
(U. Glaser sen.)

What are L-catfishes and where do they come from? Expert advice on maintenance and breeding, etc.

(48 pages + poster)
ISBN 3-931702-33-2
Item no. AS002-E

Fascinating Koi
(H. Bachmann)

A summary of the long history of colored carp, accurate guidance on maintenance and what a koi pond should be like. Plus much more useful information from an expert.

(48 pages + poster)
ISBN 3-931702-41-3
Artikel-Nr. AS003-E

Freshwater Coral Fish MALAWI cichlids
(E. Schraml)

Colorful as marine fishes, but requiring far less outlay on equipment for maintenance and breeding. Learn the secrets of success in this guide by an expert.

(48 pages + poster)
ISBN 3-931702-49-9
Item no. AS009-E

Goldfish and Fancy Goldfish
(K. H. Bernhardt)

The oldest and best-known ornamental fish, but do you realize how many forms and color varieties exist? Interesting facts on the history of these fish, plus numerous tips on their care, as they are not as hardy as often assumed.

(48 pages + poster)
ISBN 3-931702-45-6
Item no. AS008-E

Fishes of the Year The HIGHLIGHTS
(U. Glaser sen.)

Every year new fishes appear in the trade – that is what makes the aquarium hobby so exciting. All about their origin, wild or tank-bred, awards, and characteristics of these fishes. Quick, up-to-date information for every aquarist.

(48 pages + poster)
ISBN 3-931702-69-3
Item no. AS007-E

Breathtaking Rainbows
(H. Hieronimus)

The name says it all: all the colors of the rainbow. A guide to maintenance and other essential knowledge. The biotope photos show where these pretty, easy-to-keep fishes come from and how to set up a suitable aquarium.

(48 pages + poster)
ISBN 3-931702-51-0
Item no. AS004-E

Majestic Discus
(M. Göbel)

The king of fishes, dream of every aquarist! The care of these demanding fishes and lots more advice from an expert.

(48 pages + poster)
ISBN 3-931702-43-X
Item no. AS006-E

Freshwater Stingrays from South America
(R. A. Ross)

The rivers and lakes of South America are home to fishes more usually associated with the sea: stingrays. Although feared in their home waters on account of their poisonous spines, these unique fishes have caught the imagination of increasing numbers of aquarists worldwide. This book is the first comprehensive guide to the successful maintenance and breeding of these rays. Indispensable for anyone wishing to learn more about these interesting creatures or attempt to keep them.

(64 pages)
ISBN 3-931702-87-1
Item no. AS013-E

Pictorial lexicons –
all known fishes in a group

All the important information at a glance:

- **Color photos of all the fishes of a group (inc. all varieties, color and cultivated forms)**
- **Identification of any fish is accurate and easy: scientific name, hobby name, Aqualog code number**
- **Easy-to-understand text, international maintenance symbols**
- **Newly discovered fishes published as supplements: your lexicon will always remain up-to-date!**

These 3 pictorial lexicons form a compact identification guide, for the first time covering all the killifishes of the world: the official reference book for killifish fans worldwide!

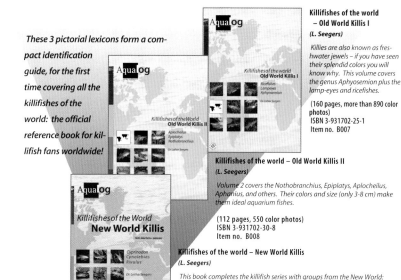

Killifishes of the world – Old World Killis I
(L. Seegers)

Killies are also known as freshwater jewels – if you have seen their splendid colors you will know why. This volume covers the genus Aphyosemion plus the lamp-eyes and ricefishes.

(160 pages, more than 890 color photos)
ISBN 3-931702-25-1
Item no. B007

Killifishes of the world – Old World Killis II
(L. Seegers)

Volume 2 covers the Nothobranchius, Epiplatys, Aplocheilus, Aphanius, and others. Their colors and size (only 3-8 cm) make them ideal aquarium fishes.

(112 pages, 550 color photos)
ISBN 3-931702-30-8
Item no. B008

Killifishes of the world – New World Killis
(L. Seegers)

This book completes the killifish series with groups from the New World: Rivulus, Cynolebias, Fundulus, Pterolebias, and others.

(224 pages, 1200 color photos)
ISBN 3-931702-76-6
Item no. B014

The Puffers
of fresh and brackish waters
(K. Ebert)

Not only 300 brilliant photos of all the puffers of the world, but more than 40 years of experience maintaining these unusual colorful creatures are shared by the author in this unique lexicon intended for the novice as well as specialist aquarists and scientists.

(96 pages, 300 color photos)
ISBN 3-931702-60-X
Item no. B016-E

All the cichlids of Latin America in 4 volumes!

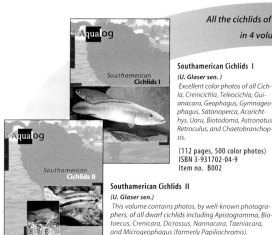

Southamerican Cichlids I
(U. Glaser sen.)
Excellent color photos of all Cichla, Crenicichla, Teleocichla, Guianacara, Geophagus, Gymnogeophagus, Satanoperca, Acarichthys, Uaru, Biotodoma, Astronotus, Retroculus, and Chaetobranchopsis.

(112 pages, 500 color photos)
ISBN 3-931702-04-9
Item no. B002

Southamerican Cichlids II
(U. Glaser sen.)
This volume contains photos, by well-known photographers, of all dwarf cichlids including Apistogramma, Biotoecus, Crenicara, Dicrossus, Nannacara, Taeniacara, and Microgeophagus (formerly Papiliochromis).

(112 pages, 500 color photos)
ISBN 3-931702-07-3
Item no. B003

Southamerican Cichlids III
(U. Glaser sen.)
In this volume you will find the catch-all genera Aequidens and Cichlasoma, plus the allied genera Acaronia, Caquetaia, Petenia, and Herotilapia. Changes in scientific names since 1988 have been taken into account.

(144 pages, 650 color photos)
ISBN 3-931702-10-3
Item no. B005

Southamerican Cichlids IV
– Discus & Scalare
(M. Göbel, H. J. Mayland)
Volume 4 covers the fantastic discus and angelfishes. Wild-caught plus German, other European, and Asian captive-bred fishes, including all varieties, color sports, and cultivated forms.

(240 pages, more than 900 color photos)
ISBN 3-931702-75-8
Item no. B010

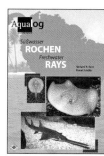

Freshwater Rays
(R. A. Ross / F. Schäfer)

All known species of freshwater rays in all their vast variety. For the first time in the history of aquarium literature a reference work including the South American fluviatile rays (Potamotrygonidae) plus the Asian, African, North American, and Australian freshwater species. Also includes the sawfishes (Pristidae) and ray species regularly found in brackish water all over the world.

(192 pages, 400 approx. color photos)
ISBN 3-931702-93-6
Item no. B015

Pictorial lexicons –
all known fishes in a group

All the important information at a glance:

- Color photos of all the fishes of a group (inc. all varieties, color and cultivated forms)
- Identification of any fish is accurate and easy: scientific name, hobby name, Aqualog code number
- Easy-to-understand text, international maintenance symbols
- Newly discovered fishes published as supplements: your lexicon will always remain up-to-date!

All rainbows
(H. Hieronimus)

All the colors of the rainbow, as the name implies. All species known to date are to be found in this book, but many more remain to be discovered in biotopes, eg in Papua New Guinea, where collecting is extremely difficult.

(144 pages, 700 approx. color photos)
ISBN 3-931702-80-4
Item no. B013

All livebearers
(M. Kempkes, F. Schäfer)

For the first time all the livebearers are illustrated – the well-known guppy, mollies, swordtails, platies, plus all the others. All the wild and cultivated forms/color varieties, as well as the halfbeaks.

(352 pages, 2000 approx. color photos)
ISBN 3-931702-77-4
Item no. B009

All Corydoras
(U. Glaser sen.)

All the mailed catfishes are presented together for the first time. As well as the genera Aspidoras, Brochis, Callichthys, Corydoras, Dianema, and Hoplosternum, there are also all variants, mutants, hybrids, cultivated forms, and undescribed species ("C-No").

(144 pages, 650 color photos)
ISBN 3-931702-13-8
Item no. B004

LORICARIIDAE – All L-Numbers
(U. Glaser sen.)

All L-number catfishes up to L204, with the rest as supplements. The only book to illustrate and describe all the L-number catfishes.

(112 pages, 450 approx. color photos)
ISBN 3-931702-01-4
Item no. B001

African Cichlids I MALAWI MBUNA
(E. Schraml)

This book really does show all mbuna species and variants covered in the lake to date!

(240 pages, 1500 approx. color photos)
ISBN 3-931702-79-0
Item no. B012

All Goldfish and Varieties
(K. H. Bernhardt)

The goldfish is the oldest ornamental fish in the world, familiar to everyone - but how many people know that there are so incredibly many varieties? This pictorial lexicon includes all the forms and color variants.

(160 pages, 690 color photos)
ISBN 3-931702-78-2
Item no. B011

All Labyrinths
(F. Schäfer)

For the first time a compact lexicon illustrating all the labyrinth fishes. Plus the snakeheads, nandids, Pristolepidae and Badidae which exhibit many behavioral parallels with the labyrinths. Also includes an identification key to the genus Betta. The official reference guide for labyrinthfish societies worldwide as soon as it was published.

(144 pages, 690 color photos)
ISBN 3-931702-21-9
Item no. B006

Book + CD-ROM

All books incl. CD-ROM

- This series of books portrays fishes of various groups using top-quality color photos
- Unambiguous identification via international code numbers, scientific and hobby names
- Brief details: Characteristics, maintenance requirements, etc.
- All photos in each book also on the accompanying CD-ROM

Version A: German, Japanese, Czech, Turkish, Hungarian
Version B: English, Dutch, Swedish, Danish, Finnish
Version C: French, Spanish, Italian, Polish, Mandarin

Photo collection No. 1
(U. Glaser sen.)
African catfishes
A: ISBN 3-931702-56-1
B: ISBN 3-931702-57-X
C: ISBN 3-931702-58-8
Item no. PC001-A/B/C

Photo collection No. 2
(U. Glaser sen.)
Characins 1
(African characins, predatory characins, pencilfishes)
A: ISBN 3-931702-59-6
B: ISBN 3-931702-62-6
C: ISBN 3-931702-63-4
Item no. PC002-A/B/C

Photo collection No. 3
(U. Glaser sen.)
Characins 2
(Piranhas, silver dollars, headstanders, hatchetfishes)
A: ISBN 3-931702-64-2
B: ISBN 3-931702-65-0
C: ISBN 3-931702-66-9
Item no. PC003-A/B/C

Photo collection No. 4
(U. Glaser sen.)
Characins 3
(Neons, Moenkhausia, can predatory characin characins)
A: ISBN 3-931702-81-2
B: ISBN 3-931702-44-8
C: ISBN 3-931702-47-2
Item no. PC004-A/B/C

Each volume contains 96-112 pages and approx. 300-400 color photos